Walk with Jesus and His Followers

Matthew Devotionals

TS Taylor

Matthew 4:12-16

And Leaving to Begin

12 Now when Jesus heard that John had been put in prison, He departed to Galilee. 13 And leaving Nazareth, He came and dwelt in Capernaum, which is by the sea, in the regions of Zebulun and Naphtali, 14 that it might be fulfilled which was spoken by Isaiah the prophet, saying:

15 "The land of Zebulun and the land of Naphtali,
By the way of the sea, beyond the Jordan,
Galilee of the Gentiles:
16 The people who sat in darkness have seen a great light,
And upon those who sat in the region and shadow of death
Light has dawned."

Jesus is about thirty years old. He has been baptized by John the Baptist in the wilderness region around the Jordan River and God the Father has spoken from heaven, "This is My beloved Son, in whom I am well pleased."

Jesus is then led by the Spirit into the wilderness and is tempted by the devil. Jesus is in the desert for forty days with no food. After his failed temptation, the devil leaves Jesus and the angels come to minister to Him.

Jesus has been out of touch with the world and now on His return He hears that John has been put into prison. Does Jesus think that He should have been there to protect His friend John? Probably not. He knows that John's imprisonment is an important step in bringing the kingdom of heaven to this time and place. Jesus leaves the town He grew up in, Nazareth, and goes further north, away from Jerusalem, into Galilee. He goes to the city of Capernaum, which is on the northern end of the Sea of Galilee. Perhaps this is to be closer to John's place of imprisonment, Machaerus, or to be closer to John' disciples. Perhaps it is to get away from the religious center, Jerusalem. Perhaps it is to get close to regular, working-class people who are open to receiving the Gospel message. This is where He meets some fishermen.

The message for you is that many times you must leave to begin. Sometimes it means moving to a new town to begin a new job. Sometimes it means leaving one family to marry into another one. Sometimes it means getting out of your comfort zone to do something new and hard. Sometimes it is like Jesus, going to a new place where you do not know anyone. But the way you begin is by leaving. Is it time for you to leave something or somewhere to get on a new path that God has for you?

Notes:

Matthew 4:23-25

Healing All Kinds

23 *And Jesus went about all Galilee, teaching in their synagogues, preaching the gospel of the kingdom, and healing all kinds of sickness and all kinds of disease among the people.* 24 *Then His fame went throughout all Syria; and they brought to Him all sick people who were afflicted with various diseases and torments, and those who were demon-possessed, epileptics, and paralytics; and He healed them.* 25 *Great multitudes followed Him—from Galilee, and from Decapolis, Jerusalem, Judea, and beyond the Jordan.*

Jacob has lived in Galilee all of his short life. For as long as he can remember he has been sick. He has few friends because no one wants to play with the "sick one." Their moms are afraid that Jacob might be contagious, even though he is sure that he is not.

His parents have recently heard of a new, travelling rabbi and they are really excited. This rabbi talks about repentance. He says that the kingdom of heaven is at hand. He is teaching about the gospel, the good news, of the kingdom. Not only that, He is healing all kinds of sicknesses and all kinds of people. He is healing old people, young people, thin people and fat people. Many people are going to hear this man called Jesus. Many are taking their sick friends to Him in the hope that He can heal them.

Jacob hears his parents whispering with each other late into the night. The next day, they tell Jacob that they are going to take him to meet the new rabbi in town, Jesus. Jacob has heard some rabbis before, but he has never met one, so he is excited but also a little afraid.

After Jesus has finished teaching about the new kingdom, He talks one-on-one with several people. Finally, it is Jacob's turn. Jesus stoops down so that He can look Jacob in the eyes. Jesus has such a compassionate face and such a calm demeanor. He treats Jacob like he is the most important person in the world. Jesus reaches out and touches Jacob and immediately Jacob feels his sickness leave him. Jacob is healed! Afterwards, Jesus smiles, blesses Jacob and then He moves on to another person who needs Him. Jacob always remembers that day, the healing, and that face. He learned that day that Jesus could heal all kinds of sicknesses and all kinds of people.

Jesus is there for us today, all of us. No one is so filled with sin that Jesus cannot forgive him. Are you ready to look into His face today to be forgiven?

Notes:

Matthew 5:13-16

Salt and Light

13 "You are the salt of the earth; but if the salt loses its flavor, how shall it be seasoned? It is then good for nothing but to be thrown out and trampled underfoot by men.

14 "You are the light of the world. A city that is set on a hill cannot be hidden. 15 Nor do they light a lamp and put it under a basket, but on a lampstand, and it gives light to all who are in the house. 16 Let your light so shine before men, that they may see your good works and glorify your Father in heaven."

Abigail is excited to be with the multitudes hearing Jesus, but she is tired of being tired all of the time. It is a big job taking care of her husband and their four sons. She feels like she is busy from morning to night.

Now Jesus is really talking about something that she can relate to, salt! Here in Capernaum, good salt is hard to come by. The salt from the Dead Sea is prevalent, but it does not taste right. Salt from the ocean has a much better flavor, but it is expensive and hard to get. Abigail will often mix real salt, the salt from the ocean, with the salt from the Dead Sea. When there is not enough real salt, it loses its flavor. It is often best to throw that out and start over again.

Talking about lights: the boys burn an oil lamp for hours almost every night. It is hard to keep enough oil in the house for their lamp. So, when they light the oil lamp, they put it in a prominent place in their home so that it gives light to everyone in the house.

What is Jesus talking about here? Salt and light? Abigail begins to understand how important salt is to life. It provides zest and flavor to their food and hence their lives. Light is important too; they cannot do their evening work without light. So of course you would not put it under a basket. How foolish!

Abigail begins to understand a few of the lessons that Jesus is teaching here. His followers are to bring zest and flavor to the lives of their neighbors, not just to their own families. She is to be a light before others. Her light is her good works. These good works are to give glory to her Father in heaven. Most importantly, as she cooks with salt every day and works every evening with light, she is to be the salt of the earth and the light of the world every day.

How about you; are you salt and light every day? What can you do today to be the salt of the earth and the light of the world?

Notes:

Matthew 5:17-20

Exceeding Righteousness

[17] "Do not think that I came to destroy the Law or the Prophets. I did not come to destroy but to fulfill. [18] For assuredly, I say to you, till heaven and earth pass away, one jot or one tittle will by no means pass from the law till all is fulfilled. [19] Whoever therefore breaks one of the least of these commandments, and teaches men so, shall be called least in the kingdom of heaven; but whoever does and teaches them, he shall be called great in the kingdom of heaven. [20] For I say to you, that unless your righteousness exceeds the righteousness of the scribes and Pharisees, you will by no means enter the kingdom of heaven."

Jesus is talking about matters of the heart. He is helping the multitudes understand their own spiritual poverty, to mourn their spiritual condition, to thirst after righteousness, to be merciful to others, and to have pure hearts. He is talking about making the disposition of their heart change their behavior. He wants everyone to be the salt of the earth, to bring zest and flavor to other's lives. Everyone is wondering what does this have to do with the Law?

Jesus makes a startling statement; He has come to fulfill the Law. What does this mean? He goes on to explain that His followers will do many good deeds; in fact their righteousness will exceed the righteousness of the scribes and the Pharisees. Jesus is saying this because His followers will do their good deeds because of the disposition of their hearts; His followers will not be like the Pharisees whom Isaiah described long ago,

"Inasmuch as these people draw near with
   their mouths
And honor Me with their lips,
But have removed their hearts far from Me,
And their fear toward Me is taught by the
   commandment of men,
Therefore, behold, I will again do a
   marvelous work
Among this people,
A marvelous work and a wonder..."
(Isaiah 29:13-14).

His followers will do a marvelous work, great and small deeds from the heart.

Where is your heart/works balance? Do you feel that most of the good works you do, you do because you ought to? Jesus is taking us away from the ought world to the joy-filled, zest world. He is teaching us to do good works from the heart so that He gets all of the glory. Do you need to reexamine your heart/works balance?

Notes:

Matthew 5:21-26

Murderous in Our Hearts

21 "You have heard that it was said to those of old, 'You shall not murder, and whoever murders will be in danger of the judgment.' 22 But I say to you that whoever is angry with his brother without a cause shall be in danger of the judgment. And whoever says to his brother, 'Raca!' shall be in danger of the council. But whoever says, 'You fool!' shall be in danger of hell fire. 23 Therefore if you bring your gift to the altar, and there remember that your brother has something against you, 24 leave your gift there before the altar, and go your way. First be reconciled to your brother, and then come and offer your gift. 25 Agree with your adversary quickly, while you are on the way with him, lest your adversary deliver you to the judge, the judge hand you over to the officer, and you be thrown into prison. 26 Assuredly, I say to you, you will by no means get out of there till you have paid the last penny."

Jesus begins this next section with murder. He is talking about one of the ten commandments. Eli begins to sit back comfortably, thinking that this section does not apply to him. Sure, he is not as righteous as one of the Pharisees, but he has never committed murder, taken someone else's life. But then, Jesus turns the talk to matters of the heart again.

"Whoever is angry with his brother without a cause shall be in danger of the judgment." Whoa, this gets Eli's attention. As long as he can remember, he has had a violent temper. Outbursts of anger and rage are common with him. His wife keeps telling him to watch his temper, as it will get him in big trouble one day; but he just cannot seem to manage to keep it under control. Eli cannot seem to tame the wild beast in his heart.

Jesus ends this section by talking about reconciliation. Eli begins to see how these might be connected ideas. First Eli needs God to tame his wild and murderous heart. He has learned that he cannot do this on his own. Second, he needs to engage in reconciliation. To be reconciled is an act of the will. It is going to someone, immediately, and talking about the problem at hand. If Eli has committed a fault, he needs to admit it right away and then ask for forgiveness. He needs to do this before he can even bring his gift to God's altar. Eli is going to need God's help to work on this.

Where are you on taming the anger and rage in your heart? Will you ask God to help you begin the act of reconciliation?

Notes:

Matthew 5:27-32

Adultery and Marriage

[27] *"You have heard that it was said to those of old, 'You shall not commit adultery.' [28] But I say to you that whoever looks at a woman to lust for her has already committed adultery with her in his heart. [29] If your right eye causes you to sin, pluck it out and cast it from you; for it is more profitable for you that one of your members perish, than for your whole body to be cast into hell. [30] And if your right hand causes you to sin, cut it off and cast it from you; for it is more profitable for you that one of your members perish, than for your whole body to be cast into hell.*

[31] *"Furthermore it has been said, 'Whoever divorces his wife, let him give her a certificate of divorce.' [32] But I say to you that whoever divorces his wife for any reason except sexual immorality causes her to commit adultery; and whoever marries a woman who is divorced commits adultery."*

Jesus continues by teaching from the ten commandments. He looks into the crowd of men and talks about lust. All of them admit to themselves that they have looked at a good-looking woman lustfully. After all, doesn't every man? Jesus goes on to say that this is the same as adultery. Every man there knows the penalty for adultery, death by stoning.

Jesus explains about the seriousness of sin. He warns about your whole body being cast into hell. He has everyone's attention now. Then, He talks about marriage. He focuses on the local custom of the day.

In Moses' day, God gave the Israelites some leniency on marriage, "When a man takes a wife and marries her, and it happens that she finds no favor in his eyes because he has found some uncleanness in her, and he writes her a certificate of divorce, puts it in her hand, and sends her out of his house..." (Deuteronomy 24:1). God did this to cover some gross infraction committed by the wife. However, men took "no favor" to mean much more than was intended. Wives were getting handed certificates of divorce for acts as small as burning dinner. The system was getting abused. After all, in the earliest days God said, "Therefore a man shall leave his father and mother and be joined to his wife, and they shall become one flesh" (Genesis 2:24). Marriage was to be a sacred vow. That is why Jesus said that the only reason for divorce was sexual immorality.

Jesus ties these two ideas together. We are not to commit lust in our hearts, as that is the same as adultery. Once we are in a committed relationship, we are to stick with it, for better or worse. This takes real work. One, to tame our roaming eyes. Two, to do the mental and emotional work to stay committed.

No matter where you are on this spectrum, are you ready to call on God for His help?

Notes:

Matthew 5:38-42

Go the Second Mile

38 *"You have heard that it was said, 'An eye for an eye and a tooth for a tooth.' 39 But I tell you not to resist an evil person. But whoever slaps you on your right cheek, turn the other to him also. 40 If anyone wants to sue you and take away your tunic, let him have your cloak also. 41 And whoever compels you to go one mile, go with him two. 42 Give to him who asks you, and from him who wants to borrow from you do not turn away."*

Ham hates the occupying Roman soldiers. He is praying that the Messiah will come and overthrow these Roman soldiers. That is one of the reasons he goes to hear this new rabbi, Jesus. Ham wants to hear what Jesus has to say about the accursed, evil Romans. Ham especially hates the Roman rule that says they can force any Jew, including Ham, to carry their packs for a mile. The Pharisees have determined that 2,000 steps make a mile, so at step 1,999 the Jew is allowed to drop the pack. Ham likes to drop the pack with a loud thud, hoping to break something inside.

Ham is then really surprised when Jesus tells everyone not to resist an evil person. He even says if you are forced to go one mile, volunteer to go a second mile, carrying their pack.

Jesus says if someone insults you by backhanding your right check with his right hand, then you should let him slap your left check. He even says you should be over generous to someone who sues you.

At first Ham is incensed by this. Ham thinks that the only way to win in this world is with rage and hate and conflict. Jesus seems to think that there is another way. Can Jesus possibly be right? Ham admits to himself that the way of rage and hatred is not working very well. Maybe Jesus is getting back to the old ways. "Hear, O Israel: The LORD our God, the LORD is one! You shall love the LORD your God with all your heart, with all your soul, and with all your strength" (Deuteronomy 6:4-5). "You shall not take vengeance, nor bear any grudge against the children of your people, but you shall love your neighbor as yourself: I am the LORD" (Leviticus 19:18).

What do you think about turning your cheek or going the second mile? How are you doing at turning your cheek and going the second mile?

Notes:

Matthew 5:43-48

Even the Tax Collectors Do That

43 "You have heard that it was said, 'You shall love your neighbor and hate your enemy.' 44 But I say to you, love your enemies, bless those who curse you, do good to those who hate you, and pray for those who spitefully use you and persecute you, 45 that you may be sons of your Father in heaven; for He makes His sun rise on the evil and on the good, and sends rain on the just and on the unjust. 46 For if you love those who love you, what reward have you? Do not even the tax collectors do the same? 47 And if you greet your brethren only, what do you do more than others? Do not even the tax collectors do so? 48 Therefore you shall be perfect, just as your Father in heaven is perfect."

Along with the occupying Roman soldiers, Ham hates the tax collectors. The tax collectors are fellow Jews who have sold themselves out to the Roman government. They set up their tax collecting booths either at the docks along the Sea of Galilee or at major intersections in the roadways. If you come near one of their tax collecting booths, they make you pay a percentage based on what product you are carrying. Ham especially hates the tax collector Matthew. Matthew always seems to know where and when Ham will be moving through the town and Matthew is there, ready to pounce.

Ham is expecting Jesus to denounce these Jewish betrayers, but Jesus tells everyone to love their enemies and even to pray for their persecutors. He goes on to say that God the Father causes the sun to shine on the evil as well as the good people. So, Jesus asks, "For if you love those who love you, what reward have you?" Loving those who already love you is no big deal. Again, if you greet only your own friends and family, big deal. Jesus then uses a very strong punch line, "Do not even the tax collectors do so?" Jesus is comparing Ham to the evil, wicked tax collectors?

Ham sees that Jesus is really turning things on their head, and yet He also wants to get everyone back to the old ways. Ham is going to have to think more about the old ways, like "If you meet your enemy's ox or his donkey going astray, you shall surely bring it back to him again. If you see the donkey of one who hates you lying under its burden...you shall surely help him with it" (Exodus 23:4-5).

How about you? Do you love only those who love you? Do you greet only your friends? Is it time to reach out to some strangers or enemies in love? What do you think will happen when you do this?

Notes:

Matthew 6:1-7

Not Before Others

[1] "Take heed that you do not do your charitable deeds before men, to be seen by them. Otherwise you have no reward from your Father in heaven. [2] Therefore, when you do a charitable deed, do not sound a trumpet before you as the hypocrites do in the synagogues and in the streets, that they may have glory from men. Assuredly, I say to you, they have their reward. [3] But when you do a charitable deed, do not let your left hand know what your right hand is doing, [4] that your charitable deed may be in secret; and your Father who sees in secret will Himself reward you openly.

[5] "And when you pray, you shall not be like the hypocrites. For they love to pray standing in the synagogues and on the corners of the streets, that they may be seen by men. Assuredly, I say to you, they have their reward. [6] But you, when you pray, go into your room, and when you have shut your door, pray to your Father who is in the secret place; and your Father who sees in secret will reward you openly. [7] And when you pray, do not use vain repetitions as the heathen do. For they think that they will be heard for their many words."

Anna loves showing off in front of her friends. When they asked her to join them to hear this new rabbi, Jesus, she quickly agreed. She is wearing her newest dress, which her grandmother helped her make. It has some wonderful, rich blue thread woven into the collar. She is really hoping that her friends notice the dress without too much prompting.

Anna is startled when Jesus begins talking about not doing deeds before other people. He says that when you do a charitable deed, don't sound off about it like Anna's father does. Jesus says that you are to do charitable deeds in secret. How strange!

Jesus goes on to admonish everyone not to make a big deal about praying in public. He describes Anna's uncle perfectly, as one who loves to stand on the street corner and pray out loudly with his hands raised up high. Jesus says that we should pray in our secret place. Again, how strange!

While Anna is puzzling over this, she remembers her grandmother telling stories about Hannah, Samuel's mother. Hannah was off by herself praying, away from everyone. Eli the priest could not hear her, but he saw her lips moving as she poured her heart out to God. God chose to hear her prayer and give her a son, Samuel. Perhaps that is what Jesus is talking about, the Father sees us praying in secret. After all, when we pray, are we not talking to Him?

How about you? Do you have a secret place where you tell your Heavenly Father everything?

Notes:

Matthew 6:9-13

Pray in This Manner

⁹ In this manner, therefore, pray:
Our Father in heaven,
Hallowed be Your name.
¹⁰ Your kingdom come.
Your will be done
On earth as it is in heaven.
¹¹ Give us this day our daily bread.
¹² And forgive us our debts,
As we forgive our debtors.
¹³ And do not lead us into temptation,
But deliver us from the evil one.
For Yours is the kingdom and the power and
    the glory forever. Amen.

Jesus continues talking about prayer by giving a sample prayer. He does not mean that we need to repeat this exact prayer over and over again, but to pray in this manner. Jesus starts His prayer by calling God Our Father. This is not the first time He has addressed God as Father; He has actually done it quite a few times. Still, it is a different way to pray. Jesus is saying that we should approach our heavenly Father as children speak to their parents with intimacy, love and admiration.

We are asked to acknowledge God Our Father who is in heaven. He is so much bigger than we are, and also bigger than our problems; He is One who has real creative power. After all, He made everything from the beginning of time. He is not only God Almighty, powerful Creator; but He is holy. Jesus is reminding everyone of the singing seraphim who cried out;

"Holy, holy, holy is the LORD of hosts;
The whole earth is full of His glory!"
(Isaiah 6:3)

God is not only Father, but He is King. He reigns over a kingdom, the kingdom of heaven. In the beginning of creation, His kingdom and the garden of Eden were one kingdom. Then when Adam and Eve rebelled against His Lordship, He banished them from the garden of Eden. Since that time, God has been redeeming His people so they can come again into His kingdom.

This is why Jesus prays that His kingdom come and His will be done here on earth. We are the ones that will do His will here on earth. The prayer is that our hearts will be made ready for God to come into them and mold them. Then our hands and feet and minds and mouths will move into action to bring about His will.

When you pray to God today, can you start by acknowledging who God is and then that He would make your heart ready so that you can be a kingdom maker?

Notes:

Matthew 6:22-23

How Great Is That Darkness

22 "The lamp of the body is the eye. If therefore your eye is good, your whole body will be full of light. 23 But if your eye is bad, your whole body will be full of darkness. If therefore the light that is in you is darkness, how great is that darkness!"

Jesus spends a great deal of time talking about issues of the heart. He says that His followers are to be the light of the world. He is talking about His followers being full of light. As Daniel is listening to this contrast of light and darkness, he remembers his own family's Passover celebration. They always talked about the nine plagues leading up to the tenth plague, where the angel of death passed over those who were protected by the blood of the lamb.

Daniel's most memorable plague is always the ninth plague, the plague of darkness.

"Then the LORD said to Moses, 'Stretch out your hand toward heaven, that there may be darkness over the land of Egypt, darkness which may even be felt.' So, Moses stretched out his hand toward heaven, and there was thick darkness in all the land of Egypt for three days. They did not see one another; nor did anyone rise from his place for three days. But all the children of Israel had light in their dwellings" (Exodus 10:21-23).

The description of this plague always frightens Daniel to his core. He has always been a little afraid of the dark, but he cannot imagine a darkness so deep and heavy that it might even be felt. This darkness is so deep that no one can see anyone else and therefore, no one moves. When thinking about this darkness, Daniel remembers a contrast from the Psalms, "Your word is a lamp to my feet and a light to my path" (Psalm 119:105). Daniel begins to see that if the lamp of your body is bad, your whole body will be full of darkness. God is to be the light for the lamp of the body.

When your heart, mind, soul, and body are far from God and His illumination, you will have trouble knowing If you are on the right path. You might even have to ask yourself, "What path am I on? Where am I headed?" If you have moved far from God, you may be in darkness. You may be experiencing how great is that darkness. It may be so dark that it can be felt. Do you need to move back into the light?

Notes:

Matthew 6:24-27

What Do You Value?

24 "No one can serve two masters; for either he will hate the one and love the other, or else he will be loyal to the one and despise the other. You cannot serve God and mammon.

25 "Therefore I say to you, do not worry about your life, what you will eat or what you will drink; nor about your body, what you will put on. Is not life more than food and the body more than clothing? 26 Look at the birds of the air, for they neither sow nor reap nor gather into barns; yet your heavenly Father feeds them. Are you not of more value than they? 27 Which of you by worrying can add one cubit to his stature?"

Jesus summarizes His previous discussion about what we treasure in our hearts by talking specifically about money and wealth, "mammon." Zibeon knows that he cannot serve two masters, his wealthy family master is enough. How could he possibly serve a second earthly master? Jesus says it is the same with our lives; we cannot serve God and our own self-centered interests. We need to see where our heart is. Jesus goes on to give everyone a visual description of heart and treasures by talking about worrying.

He starts by commanding everyone, "Do not worry." Zibeon is confused by this. His mother worries all of the time. *What will they have for dinner? Do they have enough money?* As Zibeon thinks about it, the wealthy worry about the same things. Does everyone worry all of the time? What does this say about people obeying Jesus' command, "Do not worry"?

Zibeon is sitting on the hillside with the multitudes. He looks at the birds flying overhead. To Jesus' point they seem to be well cared for and without worry. Jesus brings up value again. In this case He compares Zibeon's value to the value of the birds of the air. He says that Zibeon is much more valuable to God than the birds of the air, as Zibeon is made in God's image. Zibeon realizes that this is all about value and where we place our trust. What do we trust to keep us safe and make us happy?

On the worry-scale of one to ten, where are you today? Do you worry all of the time? Are you proud of being a worrywart? What does all of this worrying say about your relationship with God? Is it time for you to reevaluate where you have put your trust?

Notes:

Matthew 7:1-5

Speck in Your Eye

[1]*"Judge not, that you be not judged.* [2]*For with what judgment you judge, you will be judged; and with the measure you use, it will be measured back to you.* [3]*And why do you look at the speck in your brother's eye, but do not consider the plank in your own eye?* [4]*Or how can you say to your brother, 'Let me remove the speck from your eye'; and look, a plank is in your own eye?* [5]*Hypocrite! First remove the plank from your own eye, and then you will see clearly to remove the speck from your brother's eye."*

Esther comes to hear Jesus with her mother. When Jesus starts talking about specks and planks, Esther laughs out loud. There are many times that Esther gets specks of dirt in her own eyes given how dusty it is where they live. Sometimes it hurts so bad that Esther has to ask her mother to help her with the speck in her eye. She knows that her mother can help because she has bright and clear eyes.

When Esther considers the image of someone having a plank in her eye, she laughs. Her father works with wood, so he often carries a plank in his arms. But he never has a plank in his eye. Not only could he not see but he would be bumping into everyone and everything. How funny!

Esther decides that Jesus wants to teach her something serious with this funny illustration. The first part of this message is about judging others. Jesus says that Esther will be judged by the same measure that she uses against others. Uh oh, this is a problem for Esther. She often tells her sister to be more patient, when she herself is not very patient. She tells her best girl friends to be nicer to others, when she herself is sometimes not very nice.

Maybe this is what Jesus is telling Esther. She needs to clean up her own life, her attitude, and her speech. Only after she cleans up her own life can she begin to criticize others.

Esther really likes this message. Whenever she catches herself judging someone else, she is going to stop and visualize herself with a large plank sticking out of her eye. The absurdity of it all will help her to catch herself and then change her behavior.

How about you? Are you walking around with a plank in your eye? Can you use the absurdity of this image to help you be filled with love, patience and generosity for others instead of judgment?

Notes:

Matthew 7:7-11

Bread or Stones?

7 "Ask, and it will be given to you; seek, and you will find; knock, and it will be opened to you. 8 For everyone who asks receives, and he who seeks finds, and to him who knocks it will be opened. 9 Or what man is there among you who, if his son asks for bread, will give him a stone? 10 Or if he asks for a fish, will he give him a serpent? 11 If you then, being evil, know how to give good gifts to your children, how much more will your Father who is in heaven give good things to those who ask Him!"

Philp has been listening intently to Jesus for a long time. He is beginning to get hungry. Now Jesus has his attention because He is talking about bread and fish. Jesus is talking about these simple items of food in the context of asking God for things. Philip gets the idea that God can help you find things, He can open doors, and He can give good gifts. Philip notices in the beginning that Jesus is careful not to say that God will give you exactly what you ask for or exactly what you seek.

Jesus goes on to compare God's response to His people to Philip's response to his son. Philp has never given his son a stone when he asked for a piece of bread. Nor has he ever given his son a serpent instead of a fish. Sure, there have been many times where Philip has not given his son exactly what he asked for, but Philip has always given his son something good and not something that is bad for him.

Jesus then goes on to call Philip evil. Philip knows that he is not as good as God, but evil? Philip realizes that Jesus wants to get him to understand just how good God is. If Philip knows how to give good gifts to his son, how much more will God the Father know how to give good things to His children?

Philip notices that Jesus does not say that God will give him everything that he asks for, but God will give him good things. God only knows how to give good things; in fact, He knows how to give the best things.

How about you? Do you know how to give good gifts? Do you know how to ask God for good things or do you only know how to ask for things that you want? Can you think about the difference between good things and things you want in your life?

Notes:

Matthew 7:15-20

Known by Their Fruits

[15] *"Beware of false prophets, who come to you in sheep's clothing, but inwardly they are ravenous wolves.* [16] *You will know them by their fruits. Do men gather grapes from thornbushes or figs from thistles?* [17] *Even so, every good tree bears good fruit, but a bad tree bears bad fruit.* [18] *A good tree cannot bear bad fruit, nor can a bad tree bear good fruit.* [19] *Every tree that does not bear good fruit is cut down and thrown into the fire.* [20] *Therefore by their fruits you will know them."*

James has been working in the family fishing business his entire life. He really likes being on the water, in the middle of the Sea of Galilee. There is a certain freedom that comes with being in the wind and the waves. For James, his least favorite part of the job is selling their fish and haggling with the merchants on the docks. So, when Jesus starts talking about wolves in sheep's clothing, James knows exactly what Jesus is talking about. The merchants pretend to be your friend, trying to make a deal that is good for you, while all along they are only working towards a deal that is in their best interest.

It must be the same with travelling rabbis and false prophets. But, how do you tell the genuine man of God from a false one? Jesus says it is the same with merchants and prophets, you know them by their fruits. Their fruits are how they act, how they treat others; their fruits are not just what they say, but what they do.

Jesus goes on to explain it using trees. Good trees have deep roots in good soil. Good trees bear good fruit, the best fruit. Bad trees are those that do not have deep roots, that are in poor soil. And they bear bad fruit. Their fruit is not sweet. Their fruit is sour and pithy. Every tree that does not bear good fruit is to be cut down and thrown into the fire.

James gets this image immediately. Our relationship with God has little to do with our position in the religious community. Just because someone is a learned Pharisee does not mean that he is right with God. We will know whether this is true or not by his fruits.

Imagine that you have been working with a group of people for over a year. You are in the company break room and you mention that you go to church every Sunday. More than that, you say that you know Jesus as your personal savior. Will everyone be surprised by your profession of faith, or will they already know that by your fruits?

Notes:

Matthew 7:24-27

Foundation of Rock

[24] *"Therefore whoever hears these sayings of Mine, and does them, I will liken him to a wise man who built his house on the rock:* [25] *and the rain descended, the floods came, and the winds blew and beat on that house; and it did not fall, for it was founded on the rock.*

[26] *"But everyone who hears these sayings of Mine, and does not do them, will be like a foolish man who built his house on the sand:* [27] *and the rain descended, the floods came, and the winds blew and beat on that house; and it fell. And great was its fall."*

Jude has been helping friends and neighbors build homes in and around Capernaum for over twenty years. It is a hard job because the soil is so inconsistent. Some places have good solid rock only a few feet below the sandy soil. They are great places for a solid foundation on which to build a solid house. However, just fifty feet either way, the soil is sandy, with no rock for a foundation in sight. Sometimes Jude has to tell his customers that he cannot build a house on their location. They do not want to hear that. Sometimes, they get someone else to help them build their house anyway. Jude hates to see this. After all that hard work, when the hard Spring rains come, the runoff washes away the sandy soil underneath the house. If the rain storm is big enough, the house will fall.

Jude nods with approval at the illustration that Jesus is using. Jesus says that there are two parts to responding to His message. First, you have to hear what He is saying. He means you have to really hear, not just in one ear and out the other. You need to take His words into your heart, meditate on them, and see how they apply to your life. Then, you need to do something, not just sit around and listen. The doing is often the harder part. Sometimes the doing is changing some aspect of your own life. It may be changing your relationship with another person. It may be changing your relationship with God. It may be as simple as getting up early in the morning to pray and prepare for the day.

In your journey in this life, are you mostly wise or foolish? Do you have a solid foundation? Jesus is giving you a pretty good illustration of the wise person. Are you ready to be wise and to hear and do?

Notes:

Matthew 8:16-17

He Himself Took Our Infirmities

16 When evening had come, they brought to Him many who were demon-possessed. And He cast out the spirits with a word, and healed all who were sick, 17 that it might be fulfilled which was spoken by Isaiah the prophet, saying:

*"He Himself took our infirmities
And bore our sicknesses."*

It is getting to be evening in Capernaum and Jesus is still engaged in His ministry work. He is casting out demons and healing the sick. Many in the crowd are discussing whether or not this traveling rabbi, Jesus, could be the long-awaited Messiah. Everyone agrees that the Messiah will come to save His people. However, no one can agree on what "save" means. Ham, who hates the Romans, is sure that the Messiah will come to overthrow the Roman rulers. Isaac, who is tired of seeing the hypocrisy of the Pharisees, the religious leaders, thinks that the Messiah will bring true religion and worship back to God's people.

Simon sees Jesus interacting with the sick and demon possessed and he sees Jesus as the One who bore their sicknesses. Simon is reminded of Isaiah's saying of old about the Messiah being the suffering servant.

⁴ Surely He has borne our griefs
And carried our sorrows;
Yet we esteemed Him stricken,
Smitten by God, and afflicted.
⁵ But He was wounded for our transgressions,
He was bruised for our iniquities;
The chastisement for our peace was upon Him,
And by His stripes we are healed.
⁶ All we like sheep have gone astray;
We have turned, every one, to his own way;
And the LORD has laid on Him the iniquity of us
     all.
(Isaiah 53:4-6)

Simon wonders, could Jesus really be the long-awaited Messiah? He is showing that besides being a wise teacher, and a great religious rabbi, that He is also a suffering servant. Simon wonders, what does it mean that He "carried our sorrows," that He was "smitten by God" and "by His stripes we are healed"? Simon is going to need to follow Jesus more to better understand this.

How about you? In your life, do you see Jesus not only as the King of kings, but also as the One who was wounded for your transgressions? What does this aspect of Jesus' life mean to you?

Notes:

Matthew 8:23-27

Who Can This Be?

23 Now when He got into a boat, His disciples followed Him. 24 And suddenly a great tempest arose on the sea, so that the boat was covered with the waves. But He was asleep. 25 Then His disciples came to Him and awoke Him, saying, "Lord, save us! We are perishing!"

26 But He said to them, "Why are you fearful, O you of little faith?" Then He arose and rebuked the winds and the sea, and there was a great calm. 27 So the men marveled, saying, "Who can this be, that even the winds and the sea obey Him?"

It has been a long day. James is glad to get back to the boat and back on the water. He is more at home on the water than with the multitudes. Jesus is worn out, so he immediately lays His head on a pillow and goes to sleep. Everything is fine for the first part of the trip, and then a storm kicks up. To James this is no big deal, as small storms come out of nowhere on the Sea of Galilee all of the time. However, this storm is getting worse and worse. The waves are crashing over the bow of the boat.

James has seen a lot of storms, but never one this bad. He wakes Jesus up and says, "Lord, save us! We are perishing!" Jesus wakes up and asks them why they are so afraid. Jesus then stands up in the boat and rebukes the wind and the waves and tells them to be still. Immediately a great calm comes over the Sea of Galilee. James asks the other disciples, "Who can this be, that even the winds and the sea obey Him?"

Years later James enjoyed telling this story to other followers. He always told it with a gleam in his eye. Here he is, a seasoned sailor, waking up a carpenter and asking him to help them with the boat. What did he expect Jesus to do, make them a larger oar? Jesus wakes up, takes in the situation, calms the sea, and then looks at James and asks him where is his faith? James has already seen Jesus do many healing miracles. He has seen Jesus cast out demons and send them back to hell. Why is he surprised that Jesus could calm the sea?

James always remembered this as his most personal miracle. The sea was James' domain and here Jesus showed him that He is Lord over everything in James' life. This was the first time that James really understood who Jesus was, Lord over all.

How about you? When you are in your boat in the midst of a storm what do you do, paddle harder? If you were to pray, "Lord, save me," would you be surprised when He did? What would He say about your faith?

Notes:

Matthew 8:28-29

Before the Time

28 When He had come to the other side, to the country of the Gergesenes, there met Him two demon-possessed men, coming out of the tombs, exceedingly fierce, so that no one could pass that way. 29 And suddenly they cried out, saying, "What have we to do with You, Jesus, You Son of God? Have You come here to torment us before the time?"

The disciples made it to the other side of the Sea of Galilee with Jesus and they were immediately confronted by two demon-possessed men. These were two bad news characters. They lived in a cemetery among the tombs and they were fierce. When they saw Jesus, the demons who possessed the men cried out "Have you come here to torment us before the time?"

This is an incredibly important declaration by the demons. First, they recognize Jesus for who He is. He is the Lord of lords and He has authority over the demons as well as the wind and waves. He is the Son of God and comes with the full authority of God the Father. Second, they recognize that Jesus has the power and authority to torment them. The demons know that they are at war with the holy One and He can overpower them and torment them.

Most important, they know that there is a time for their demise. They know that they are in a spiritual war and they know for sure that they are going to lose the war. They know that they and their master, Satan, will be defeated. They know that they will be cast into hell and tormented forever. Even though they know that they will lose the war, they continue to fight a losing battle. At this time, they know that it is not the end of their time, so they ask Jesus if He will torment them before the time. They know that He has the power and authority to choose the time of their torment.

John foretells the time of their final defeat;

"Alleluia! Salvation and glory and honor and power belong to the Lord our God! For true and righteous are His judgments, because He has judged the great harlot who corrupted the earth with her fornication; and He has avenged on her the blood of His servants shed by her." Again they said, "Alleluia! Her smoke rises up forever and ever!"
(Revelation 19:1b-3).

Know this, there is a spiritual war going on around you. You do not have the power to cast out or torment the demons, only Jesus does, and He will be the ultimate victor. How will you live your life differently knowing that there is a time when evil will be defeated?

Notes:

Matthew 9:1-7

Your Sins Are Forgiven

¹ So He got into a boat, crossed over, and came to His own city. ² Then behold, they brought to Him a paralytic lying on a bed. When Jesus saw their faith, He said to the paralytic, "Son, be of good cheer; your sins are forgiven you."

³ And at once some of the scribes said within themselves, "This Man blasphemes!"

⁴ But Jesus, knowing their thoughts, said, "Why do you think evil in your hearts? ⁵ For which is easier, to say, 'Your sins are forgiven you,' or to say, 'Arise and walk'? ⁶ But that you may know that the Son of Man has power on earth to forgive sins"—then He said to the paralytic, "Arise, take up your bed, and go to your house." ⁷ And he arose and departed to his house.

Jesus was teaching in a house to a large group of people. There were regular members of the local synagogue as well as a few of the religious leaders, the scribes. Several men were concerned about their best friend, Reuben, who had been paralyzed in a construction accident. The house was so filled with the crowd that they could not get Reuben inside to see Jesus. Not to be thwarted, they went up to the roof and made a Reuben-sized hole in the roof, lowered him down in front of Jesus. Jesus looks up at them as they stare down at Him through the hole and He is impressed by their faith.

Jesus then turns His attention to Reuben. He does not ask Rueben about his faith, nor does He ask Reuben what he wants, He just declares, "Be of good cheer." At first Reuben is taken aback by this, what does he have to be cheerful about? He is embarrassed to be lying in front of the rabbi and the crowd, totally exposed. Then Jesus says to Reuben that his sins are forgiven. At first Reuben is confused by this proclamation and then he feels a great peace wash over him. All of a sudden, all of his anger, hatred, guilt, and depression are gone. He feels clean for the first time and he realizes that Jesus has taken care of his real problem.

However, the scribes are very unhappy with this. They are thinking, *Who does Jesus think He is? Only God can forgive sins.* Jesus knows what they are thinking and so He shows them that He has the authority and power to forgive sin with a visual demonstration. Jesus tells Reuben to get up and walk home. Reuben cannot believe it; his legs are working again. He does not just walk, but he runs and skips home, not just because he can walk, but because he has been made clean.

So it is with you. Jesus came to die for your sins so that they may be forgiven once and for all. Is it time for you to ask for forgiveness for some of those paralyzing sins and then get up and run knowing the peace that passes all understanding?

Notes:

Matthew 9:9-13

I Call Them to Repentance

9 As Jesus passed on from there, He saw a man named Matthew sitting at the tax office. And He said to him, "Follow Me." So he arose and followed Him.

10 Now it happened, as Jesus sat at the table in the house, that behold, many tax collectors and sinners came and sat down with Him and His disciples. 11 And when the Pharisees saw it, they said to His disciples, "Why does your Teacher eat with tax collectors and sinners?"

12 When Jesus heard that, He said to them, "Those who are well have no need of a physician, but those who are sick. 13 But go and learn what this means: 'I desire mercy and not sacrifice.' For I did not come to call the righteous, but sinners, to repentance."

A little later, Jesus comes upon Matthew the tax collector confronting Ham over his taxes. Ham is ecstatic when he sees Jesus appear at Matthew's tax office. Finally, the rabbi is going to give this Jewish traitor tax collector what's coming to him. However, Jesus and Matthew have a short, quiet conversation and then Jesus says, "Follow Me." Ham wonders what is going on. Jesus wants the despicable tax collector to be one of His disciples?

A few days later, Ham comes upon a big party in the neighborhood. It turns out that the party is at Matthew's house. Matthew is there with many of his tax collector friends and Ham sees Jesus in among them having a good time. Ham is like some of the Pharisees nearby. They are asking everyone, "What is Jesus doing eating with these despicable tax collectors? They are unclean sinners!"

Jesus hears them and He asks them a simple, question something like, "Who goes to the physician, the well or the sick? "As the Pharisees mull this over, Jesus continues, "For I did not come to call the righteous, but sinners, to repentance." Ham catches the irony in Jesus' message. Neither he nor the Pharisees are really righteous. Ham is too focused on going through the religious motions, instead of being merciful to people like Matthew. Matthew saw his great need for repentance and he left his old life to follow Jesus. Not only did he follow Jesus, but he had a big party to introduce many of his friends to Jesus. Matthew wanted to show his friends the fruits of his repentance.

How about you? Are you ready to throw a Matthew party? Invite some friends who do not know Jesus and just have a good time with them. Get to know them and find ways to show mercy. Why not start making your invitation list today?

Notes:

Matthew 9:18-19, 23-26

Took Her by the Hand

18 While He spoke these things to them, behold, a ruler came and worshiped Him, saying, "My daughter has just died, but come and lay Your hand on her and she will live." 19 So Jesus arose and followed him, and so did His disciples.

23 When Jesus came into the ruler's house, and saw the flute players and the noisy crowd wailing, 24 He said to them, "Make room, for the girl is not dead, but sleeping." And they ridiculed Him. 25 But when the crowd was put outside, He went in and took her by the hand, and the girl arose. 26 And the report of this went out into all that land.

Jesus is talking about how His followers will live changed lives. They will be like new wine in new wineskins, full of love and joy. While He is speaking, a ruler from the local synagogue, an important scribe, comes before Him. The ruler tells Jesus that his daughter has just died. He asks Jesus to lay His hands on her so that she will live, be resurrected from the dead! He is a bit surprised that this Jewish ruler would expect Him to do this as the rulers are typically at odds with Jesus and His message. However, Jesus feels the ruler's pain, so He goes with the ruler to his house.

When Jesus arrives at the rulers' house, He sees that the mourning ceremony has already started. In Jesus' day, mourning the dead was a big deal, almost as big a deal as a wedding. Typically, the family would hire professional musicians and lamenters to mourn the loss of their loved one. The greater their loss, the bigger the mourning ceremony.

Jesus tells them that the girl is not dead. If there is one thing that a professional mourner knows, it is if the person is dead or not. They have seen many cold bodies where rigor mortis has set it. So, they ridicule this young, travelling rabbi. Jesus asks that the mourners be sent outside of the house so that He can be with the girl.

The father goes into the room and sees Jesus say a few quiet words over his daughter. Then the most amazing thing happens, Jesus takes the daughter by the hand. Jesus takes her hand like any father would take his child's hand to help her up. It is a gentle, patient, and compassionate move. The daughter opens her eyes, looks into the face of Jesus, similes, and gets up. Then she runs into her father's arms.

Jesus stands ready to take your hand. He is ready to pull you out of your old, dead life. He is ready to take you into a new life, full of love and joy. Are you ready to take His hand and arise?

Notes:

Matthew 9:20-23

Who Is Important Enough?

20 And suddenly, a woman who had a flow of blood for twelve years came from behind and touched the hem of His garment. 21 For she said to herself, "If only I may touch His garment, I shall be made well." 22 But Jesus turned around, and when He saw her He said, "Be of good cheer, daughter; your faith has made you well." And the woman was made well from that hour.

Jesus is on a mission to heal the daughter of an important ruler of the local synagogue, and not just heal, but raise from the dead. This is unprecedented. A "super miracle" and not just for anyone, but for a scribe, a ruler of the synagogue. The disciples are talking among themselves about this finally being their chance to break into the big time. If Jesus does a great miracle for this important Jewish ruler, perhaps they will all get the recognition that they deserve. Perhaps now, when they visit a town, they will get to stay in the nicest houses instead of either sleeping out in the open or with the very poor. James and John, the sons of Zebedee, were particularly excited about the improvement in their social standing.

Then for seemingly no reason, Jesus stops and turns around. When Jesus says that someone touched the hem of His garment, James and John almost lose it entirely. They say to themselves something like; *What does He mean, 'Who touched my hem?' There are lots of people jostling into us. What could Jesus possibly mean?* Jesus then picks out a sickly, poor woman of low esteem and looks her in the eyes and speaks with her. James and John are thinking, *Doesn't Jesus get it that this ailing woman is nothing compared to the ruler of the synagogue?* Jesus still takes His time with this woman and tells her that her faith has made her well.

Finally, they get back on the main mission to help the important religious ruler. Do you suppose that Jesus spoke to the disciples that night about who is important? Do you suppose that Jesus spoke with them about the "least of these," about anyone and everyone being able to come to Him?

Where do you place yourself in this story? Are you the important religious person, are you James, or are you the suffering woman? Are you hesitant to reach out to Jesus because you are not important enough? Is it time to reconsider this?

Notes:

Matthew 9:27-31

Be Persistent

27 When Jesus departed from there, two blind men followed Him, crying out and saying, "Son of David, have mercy on us!"

28 And when He had come into the house, the blind men came to Him. And Jesus said to them, "Do you believe that I am able to do this?"

They said to Him, "Yes, Lord."

29 Then He touched their eyes, saying, "According to your faith let it be to you." 30 And their eyes were opened. And Jesus sternly warned them, saying, "See that no one knows it." 31 But when they had departed, they spread the news about Him in all that country.

Jesus is a travelling rabbi. He has no home church or congregation. He is always traveling from town to town preaching and healing. One day on His journey, two blind men are following Him. This in itself is no small feat. Blind men would usually sit in one location and beg for food or money. That was a pretty horrible existence. In this case, however, these two blind men were committed to the task of receiving mercy from Jesus, so they made the bold choice to follow Him.

Even though the two blind men were crying out to Jesus, He did not acknowledge their cries. We do not know why He seemed to ignore them. Perhaps the disciples were talking to Him and demanding His full attention. Perhaps He knew it was not time to minister to these blind men. We just do not know, but we do know that they persisted in their cries.

The blind men followed Jesus and His disciples along the path into town. Somehow, they figured out the exact house where Jesus was staying. They found their way to the front door and made their way into the house where Jesus was teaching. They had been calling Jesus by His Messianic name, Son of David, asking for mercy. Jesus asked a somewhat rhetorical question, "Do you believe that I am able to do this?" In this case their actions spoke louder than their words, "Yes, Lord." Jesus then reached out and touched their eyes and healed them.

Sometimes God asks us to be patient and persistent. There are times when He does not answer our prayers with anything other than "Not now." He never fully explains to us why we need to wait, but perhaps one reason is to teach us to be persistent.

The next time God tells you, "Not now" and asks you to wait, can you remember these two blind men and remain persistent?

Notes:

Matthew 9:32-34

They Will Call Good Evil

32 As they went out, behold, they brought to Him a man, mute and demon-possessed. 33 And when the demon was cast out, the mute spoke. And the multitudes marveled, saying, "It was never seen like this in Israel!"

34 But the Pharisees said, "He casts out demons by the ruler of the demons."

Jesus leaves the area where He healed the two blind men who are now greatly rejoicing. Some of the multitudes bring a man who is mute and demon-possessed. When the demon is cast out of the man, he begins to speak and praise God, much like John the Baptist's father who had been mute for nine months, until his tongue was loosed and he spoke, praising God. Even the multitudes marvel at these great, miraculous deeds of Jesus.

But the Pharisees are not buying into this. They are the religious leaders of the day and they are feeling threatened. They do not know how to deal with Jesus—their power and influence is threatened by His popularity. They cannot do the great deeds that He does nor can they make Him stop. So, they come up with a plan to undermine Him. They spread the rumor that He casts out demons by the power of the ruler of the demons.

Most of the people do not buy into this idea. Some of them have even seen the demons acknowledge

Jesus' power and authority over them. The people recall the words of the prophet Isaiah;

20 *Woe to those who call evil good, and good evil;*
Who put darkness for light, and light for darkness;
Who put bitter for sweet, and sweet for bitter!
21 *Woe to those who are wise in their own eyes,*
And prudent in their own sight!
(Isaiah 5:20-21)

This is so like us today. People do not like how things are going. They are fighting for power and influence. When they cannot do great deeds on their own, they begin to call evil good, and good evil. When you see this happening, what will you do? Will you remain quiet and hidden in the crowd, or will you stand up for what is right and bravely speak the truth?

Notes:

Matthew 9:35-38

The Lord of the Harvest

35 Then Jesus went about all the cities and villages, teaching in their synagogues, preaching the gospel of the kingdom, and healing every sickness and every disease among the people. 36 But when He saw the multitudes, He was moved with compassion for them, because they were weary and scattered, like sheep having no shepherd. 37 Then He said to His disciples, "The harvest truly is plentiful, but the laborers are few. 38 Therefore pray the Lord of the harvest to send out laborers into His harvest."

Jesus has been traveling throughout the northern cities and villages. Everywhere He goes He preaches the gospel of the kingdom. He tells everyone that they need to be convicted of their spiritual poverty, they need to mourn over their sins, they need to hunger and thirst for righteousness, and they need to be pure in heart. Everywhere He goes, He heals all kinds of sickness and disease. But when He looks at the needs of the multitudes, He is moved with compassion. The multitudes look and act like sheep moving around without a shepherd. They do not seem to understand their purpose in life. They do not know where they are headed. They have no clue how to seek first the kingdom of God. For His message to reach more lost sheep, He needs more laborers to send out to harvest more lives.

This is one of the few times when Jesus tells His disciples to pray and what and to whom to pray. The disciples are to pray to God the Father, the Lord of the harvest, to send out more laborers. The most important step in sending out laborers is not the sending, but the changing of their hearts so that they are willing to be sent. It is like when Isaiah saw the Lord sitting on His throne.

Also I heard the voice of the Lord, saying: "Whom shall I send, And who will go for Us?" Then I said, "Here am I! Send me." (Isaiah 6:8)

The second important step is for the laborers to understand that they will not be going alone. God, the Holy Spirit, will go with them. He will give them strength, wisdom, love, and the words to say. At the end of Matthew's gospel, he records Jesus telling His disciples, "And lo, I am with you always, even to the end of the age."

This is what it takes to be laborers in His harvest - have a changed heart to be ready, and then be willing to go, knowing in your heart that you do not go alone. Jesus will go with you even to the end of the age. Are you ready to join the laborers? It is really not that hard; you can do it!

Notes:

Matthew 10:16-20

Do Not Worry How You Should Speak

16 "Behold, I send you out as sheep in the midst of wolves. Therefore be wise as serpents and harmless as doves. 17 But beware of men, for they will deliver you up to councils and scourge you in their synagogues. 18 You will be brought before governors and kings for My sake, as a testimony to them and to the Gentiles. 19 But when they deliver you up, do not worry about how or what you should speak. For it will be given to you in that hour what you should speak; 20 for it is not you who speak, but the Spirit of your Father who speaks in you."

Jesus continues to instruct His disciples to prepare them for their missionary journeys. He says that it is going to be pretty tough, like going out into a pack of wolves. The disciples have already seen this with the religious establishment, the Pharisees, trying to call good evil, and evil good. Jesus tells them that they are going to need to be tough and smart. He describes them as wise serpents, not poisonous snakes. Their love and mercy will be so obvious that they will appear to be as harmless as doves.

Jesus does not say, "If they deliver you up," but "When." Jesus tells them that they will have to go before the religious authorities. They will be judged by very learned scholars and religious experts. They will even go before the political leaders, typically people who know how to ask complex and damning questions.

The disciples will go before these rulers to be a testimony. They will be a testimony to the person of Christ, to His mission, and to His kingdom. They all remember when the tabernacle was built.

And you shall hang the veil from the clasps. Then you shall bring the ark of the Testimony in there, behind the veil. The veil shall be a divider for you between the holy place and the Most Holy.
(Exodus 26:33)

The disciple's biggest concern is what they will say as a testimony. They are not learned religious scholars, nor are they people who have climbed the political ladder, often stepping on others to get to their exalted position. Jesus tells them not to worry. The disciples must be thinking, *Is He kidding? Don't worry?* Jesus tells them why. The appropriate words will be given to them. The Holy Spirit will indwell them and He will help them speak.

It is the same today. We are to be a testimony for Jesus. Sometimes with our lives, and sometimes with our words. When you get into a situation where you need to speak, just ask the Holy Spirit for His assistance. Can you do that?

Notes:

Matthew 10:27-31

Do Not Fear, You Are More Valuable

27 "Whatever I tell you in the dark, speak in the light; and what you hear in the ear, preach on the housetops. 28 And do not fear those who kill the body but cannot kill the soul. But rather fear Him who is able to destroy both soul and body in hell. 29 Are not two sparrows sold for a copper coin? And not one of them falls to the ground apart from your Father's will. 30 But the very hairs of your head are all numbered. 31 Do not fear therefore; you are of more value than many sparrows."

Jesus continues to tell His disciples about being a testimony to Him. He tells them not to be afraid to speak out, even from the housetops. He then goes on to explain about their value to the Father.

First, Jesus talks about the Father's care for His creation. We often forget that He is Lord and Master of all of the created world and that He is intimately involved in its upkeep and care. Jesus may be referring to some of the statements about the Father's care in the book of Job.

Have you commanded the morning since your days began,
And caused the dawn to know its place...
(Job 38:12)

Who provides food for the raven,
When its young ones cry to God,
And wander about for lack of food?
(Job 38:41)

Do you know the time when the wild
      mountain goats bear young?
Or can you mark when the deer gives birth?
(Job 39:1)

God values and cares for all of His creation, yet Jesus reminds His disciples, as valuable as the birds of the air are, they are much more valuable to God. After all, we are His image-bearers, when we go out into the world to represent God, He will be with us. However, notice that He does not say that this means we will avoid hard times. We may be brought before the courts. We may be thrown into jail. We may even be killed. But no one can kill our soul, because God is with us.

When things are tough for you and you are lost in your own pity, remember; "you are of more value." If God the Father values you, what else can really matter?

Notes:

Matthew 10:34-39

Lose and Find

34 "Do not think that I came to bring peace on earth. I did not come to bring peace but a sword. 35 For I have come to 'set a man against his father, a daughter against her mother, and a daughter-in-law against her mother-in-law'; 36 and 'a man's enemies will be those of his own household.' 37 He who loves father or mother more than Me is not worthy of Me. And he who loves son or daughter more than Me is not worthy of Me. 38 And he who does not take his cross and follow after Me is not worthy of Me. 39 He who finds his life will lose it, and he who loses his life for My sake will find it."

Isaac has been following Jesus for a while. He is very interested in understanding the teachings of Jesus compared to those of the Pharisees. Isaac is very surprised when Jesus says that He did not come to bring peace. Didn't He talk earlier about His followers being peacemakers?

Then Isaac realizes that Jesus is referring to the prophet Micah;

6 For son dishonors father,
Daughter rises against her mother,
Daughter-in-law against her mother-in-law;
A man's enemies are the men of his own
*   household.*

7 Therefore I will look to the LORD;
I will wait for the God of my salvation;
My God will hear me.
(Micah 7:6-7)

The prophet Micah was lamenting the time when Israel needed to repent from her sins. It was a time when righteousness was not found in the land.

Jesus is applying this lesson to His day and to all of His people, including the Pharisees. It is time for everyone to realize that the love for God is lacking in their lives. Everyone has put love of things, personal power, social influence, and even love for family ahead of their love for God. They all know by heart the greatest commandment: "You shall love the LORD your God with all your heart, with all your soul, and with all your strength." (Deuteronomy 6:5) And yet, they realize they have lost their first love, the LORD.

Jesus ends with a curious phrase about taking up the cross. Isaac does not know what He means. Is Jesus talking about dying like a common criminal? Surely not! Jesus summarizes with the idea that whoever loses his life for Jesus' sake and His way will find a deeper, richer life.

How about you? What do you truly value? What are you willing to die for? What will you give up, lose, to find a life full of love and joy?

Notes:

Matthew 11:1-6

Are You the Coming One?

¹ Now it came to pass, when Jesus finished commanding His twelve disciples, that He departed from there to teach and to preach in their cities.

² And when John had heard in prison about the works of Christ, he sent two of his disciples ³ and said to Him, "Are You the Coming One, or do we look for another?"

⁴ Jesus answered and said to them, "Go and tell John the things which you hear and see: ⁵ The blind see and the lame walk; the lepers are cleansed and the deaf hear; the dead are raised up and the poor have the gospel preached to them. ⁶ And blessed is he who is not offended because of Me."

John the Baptist began his ministry in the desert. He knew that God had chosen him to call the people into repentance in preparation for the coming Messiah. In fact, John called them to bear fruit worthy of repentance to show that their repentance was real. John also knew that he was the voice crying in the wilderness, "Prepare the way of the LORD" (Matthew 3:3).

John has been a faithful servant of God. He is the one who baptized Jesus and recognized Him, "Behold! The Lamb of God who takes away the sin of the world!" (John 1:29b). John also faithfully called out the tetrarch Herod for marrying his brother's wife. This is what got John thrown into prison.

John has been languishing in prison for a while and he is going through what many of us go through, a season of doubt. He must be thinking, *Was all of my ministry done in vain? Did any of it really matter?* So, he sends two of his disciples to meet Jesus and ask Him, "Are you the Coming One?"

Jesus does not chastise John for going through a season of doubt. Jesus tells the men to return to John with some encouraging words, tell him what is happening. Jesus quotes from the prophet Isaiah about the works of the Messiah. Many people have agreed with Nicodemus who said, "We know that You are a teacher from God; for no one can do these signs that You do unless God is with him." (John 3:2b) Jesus uses His miraculous healing acts as a sign pointing to His Messiahship. Yes, He is the Coming One.

You do not need to look for another. He has come as the Lamb of God who takes away your sin. He is the One who has come to help you see the best path to walk. Can you tell the people in your life that He is indeed the Coming One? There is no need to look for another.

Notes:

Matthew 11:9-15

I Send My Messenger

⁹ But what did you go out to see? A prophet? Yes, I say to you, and more than a prophet. ¹⁰ For this is he of whom it is written:

'Behold, I send My messenger before Your face,
Who will prepare Your way before You.'

¹¹ "Assuredly, I say to you, among those born of women there has not risen one greater than John the Baptist; but he who is least in the kingdom of heaven is greater than he. ¹² And from the days of John the Baptist until now the kingdom of heaven suffers violence, and the violent take it by force. ¹³ For all the prophets and the law prophesied until John. ¹⁴ And if you are willing to receive it, he is Elijah who is to come. ¹⁵ He who has ears to hear, let him hear!"

Jesus continues to talk to the multitudes about John the Baptist. He asks them, when you went into the wilderness, what did you expect to see? A prophet dressed in fine clothes and eating rich food? No, he was a messenger sent to prepare the way.

The multitudes were very excited when John first appeared on the scene because there had not been a prophet of God for over four hundred years.

The people were wondering if God had abandoned them. They were also wondering when God's prophet finally appeared, would they recognize him? They know that the last prophet of old, Malachi, said that God would "Send you Elijah the prophet." (Malachi 4:5) Everyone wondered if that meant that Elijah would be resurrected to come back in human form, or would he come as an angel, or would someone come in the spirit and power of Elijah?

When the angel Gabriel appeared to John's father, Zacharias, he told Zacharias that he and his wife Elizabeth would have a son. This son will be great in the sight of the Lord. He will be filled with the Holy Spirit. "He will also go before Him in the spirit and power of Elijah." (Luke 1:17a)

This is a great story which shows God working through four hundred years of history to bring about His plan. We should take heart from this story. God continually reminds His people that He is in charge, He is the Sovereign One.

He is always working out His plan through your life. Who knows, perhaps your great, great, granddaughter will play a pivotal role in God's kingdom many years from now. So do not lose heart, God is always at work. He is always preparing to send His messenger. Are you ready to play your part?

Notes:

Matthew 11:28-30

Easy and Light

28 "Come to Me, all you who labor and are heavy laden, and I will give you rest. 29 Take My yoke upon you and learn from Me, for I am gentle and lowly in heart, and you will find rest for your souls. 30 For My yoke is easy and My burden is light."

James is becoming weary with all of this travelling with Jesus throughout various towns and villages. It seems that every day there is a new village or two. James is used to spending much of his day in a boat on the Sea of Galilee. He is not used to walking this much. However, he would not trade the last several months for anything. Hearing Jesus teach about the kingdom of God and seeing all of these miracles. Wow, each day brings new wonderful surprises. It makes all of the walking worthwhile.

Today, Jesus is talking about resting. Hallelujah! James could do with a rest. However, there is a twist to Jesus' rest. He says, "Take My yoke upon you." While James is a sailor and fisherman, he knows enough about framing to know that a yoke is for oxen. The yoke is built for a team of two oxen. It is designed for hard work.

This is much like rowing with a partner on the sea. If you have a strong and well-matched rowing partner it feels almost effortless. James surmises that Jesus must be talking about the same kind of thing with His yoke. Only in this case, James' yoke partner will not be his brother Peter, it will be Jesus Himself. Not only will Jesus be pulling in his yoke, but James will also be learning from Him. James will be learning as he helps to build the kingdom of God. Yes, it will be work; probably hard work, but in one sense it will be an easy and light burden.

This is how it is when you are doing exactly what God wants you to do. You are paired with Jesus Himself. He is pulling on the yoke of life with you. Sure, it will be hard work sometimes, but it will also be a joy-filled life. "Seek first the kingdom of God and His righteousness, and all these things shall be added to you." Are you ready to get into the yoke?

Notes:

Matthew 12:15-21

A Bruised Reed

15 But when Jesus knew it, He withdrew from there. And great multitudes followed Him, and He healed them all. 16 Yet He warned them not to make Him known, 17 that it might be fulfilled which was spoken by Isaiah the prophet, saying:

18 "Behold! My Servant whom I have chosen,
My Beloved in whom My soul is well pleased!
I will put My Spirit upon Him,
And He will declare justice to the Gentiles.
19 He will not quarrel nor cry out,
Nor will anyone hear His voice in the streets.
20 A bruised reed He will not break,
And smoking flax He will not quench,
Till He sends forth justice to victory;
21 And in His name Gentiles will trust."

Jesus knows that the Pharisees are plotting to destroy Him. So, He moves on to a new town, but the multitudes still follow Him. Anna is following with the multitudes. When she hears Jesus describing Himself as "My Servant whom I have chosen," she is all ears. Anna gets confused, however, when Jesus starts talking about justice to the Gentiles.

Anna was told all of her life to stay away from the Gentiles. They are not God's people, they are not clean people, they do not follow the Jewish way. All of Anna's friends are Jewish, she doesn't even know any Gentiles. Even when she has seen them on the streets, she has never spoken to them. Now here is the travelling rabbi saying that the Gentiles are equal to the Jews in that He is reaching out to them and they will trust Him.

This is turning Anna's world upside down. If God's Beloved is coming to declare justice to the Gentiles and they will trust Him, does that mean that Anna will have to be friendly to the Gentile girls? Will she need to reach out and become friends with one of them? Will she need to eat lunch with one of them at school? If she does this, what will her Jewish friends think of her? Will she be totally ostracized? Anna takes heart; if she gets bruised by her friends for reaching out to others who are very different from her, so be it. She will trust Jesus.

How about you? Are you ready to reach out to someone who is different from you? Perhaps they come from a different town, a different country, or a different family structure. Perhaps they have a different skin color or they learned a different language? Can you go anyway, even if you get bruised for the effort?

Notes:

Matthew 12:22-26

A Kingdom Divided

22 Then one was brought to Him who was demon-possessed, blind and mute; and He healed him, so that the blind and mute man both spoke and saw. 23 And all the multitudes were amazed and said, "Could this be the Son of David?"

24 Now when the Pharisees heard it they said, "This fellow does not cast out demons except by Beelzebub, the ruler of the demons."

25 But Jesus knew their thoughts, and said to them: "Every kingdom divided against itself is brought to desolation, and every city or house divided against itself will not stand. 26 If Satan casts out Satan, he is divided against himself. How then will his kingdom stand?"

Jesus continues to do great deeds. He has just healed a man who was demon-possessed, rendering him blind and mute. The multitudes are coming to believe that Jesus may be the long-awaited Messiah, the Son of David. The Pharisees cannot bear to hear this. They start the rumor that Jesus is getting His power from Beelzebub, the ruler of the demons.

Jude is among the multitudes and believes that the Pharisees have lost their minds from jealousy. He knows from his construction business that you cannot accomplish anything when your efforts are divided like this. Jude sees this like building a house half on a foundation of rock and half on a foundation of sand. The whole structure would be continually fighting against itself and it would collapse.

Jude agrees with Jesus when He says, "Every city or house divided against itself will not stand." Jude sees the Pharisees trying to do this, not Jesus. They are trying to turn the multitudes against Jesus for their own political purposes. Don't they see that they are in danger of causing the destruction of the whole religious structure? Divided it will not stand!

Jude thinks that this is the time for all sides to come together for a reasoned discussion; however, if all of the sides cannot agree, Jude cannot choose any side but Jesus'. He is the One with the great teaching, focused on heart changes. He is teaching about doing good. He is focused on building the kingdom of God. Jude wants to build with Him.

The same can be true today. Jesus' followers focus on their own agenda, their own view of the world, and their own view of what is most important to do. Sometimes they take their eyes off of Jesus and they only focus on dividing the kingdom of God. When you see this happening around you, can you say "Stop"? It is time to stop dividing the kingdom of God.

Notes:

Matthew 12:33-35

Out of the Treasure of the Heart

33 "Either make the tree good and its fruit good, or else make the tree bad and its fruit bad; for a tree is known by its fruit. 34 Brood of vipers! How can you, being evil, speak good things? For out of the abundance of the heart the mouth speaks. 35 A good man out of the good treasure of his heart brings forth good things, and an evil man out of the evil treasure brings forth evil things."

Eli has been following and listening to Jesus for a number of days. Eli is hoping that Jesus will give Eli the key to controlling his anger. At first Eli is frustrated by Jesus' teaching about good and bad trees. Eli is thinking, *What do trees have to do with us?* Then, he begins to understand that it is not just about the tree, its trunk, branches and leaves, but it is about the fruit produced by the tree.

Jesus rails against the Pharisees, calling them vipers and evil. This is because they do not show good fruit: genuine, self-sacrificing deeds from the heart. Jesus then focuses on the abundance of the heart which is the source of our words, both good and bad, as well as our deeds.

Eli thinks back to some of the wisdom proverbs about fools, people who despise wisdom and instruction. Fools do not fill their hearts and minds with the things of God, just with the folly of the world. Eli thinks that Jesus is referring to the Pharisees from Proverbs 10:23: "To do evil is like sport to a fool."

Then, Eli begins to think that Jesus is talking directly to him as he recalls Proverbs 18:6-7:

A fool's lips enter into contention,
And his mouth calls for blows.
A fool's mouth is his destruction,
And his lips are the snare of his soul.

He begins to see that it is all a matter of the heart: "A good man out of the good treasure of this heart brings forth good things." Eli sees that if he wants to get rid of his anger, he will need a new heart. He knows that he cannot change his heart on his own, he needs Jesus to give him a new heart. To nurture this new heart, Eli will need to cling to the words of Jesus. Perhaps he will start by hungering and thirsting after this new treasure in his heart.

So it is with us. We cannot change our own hearts. Only Jesus can do that. Are you ready to ask Jesus to change your heart and the treasure of your heart? If you would like help with a prayer, there is one at the end of the book.

Notes:

Matthew 12:38-40

Give Us a Sign

38 Then some of the scribes and Pharisees answered, saying, "Teacher, we want to see a sign from You."

39 But He answered and said to them, "An evil and adulterous generation seeks after a sign, and no sign will be given to it except the sign of the prophet Jonah. 40 For as Jonah was three days and three nights in the belly of the great fish, so will the Son of Man be three days and three nights in the heart of the earth."

Esther is still following Jesus and listening to His light-hearted, humorous sayings. In this case, she laughs at the scribes and Pharisees. She hears them saying, "Teacher, we want to see a sign from You." Esther is thinking that they must be blind. How many miracles does Jesus need to do for them to believe? Jesus did call them blind guides, so maybe He is poking fun at them too.

She then hears Jesus referring to the sign of Jonah. Jonah is one of her favorite stories. It not only shows God's care for His people, in this case the prophet Jonah, but God's creativity and imagination are shown by the way He saves Jonah. She is sure that years later Jonah chuckled over the fact that God used a great fish to save him. Who would have even thought of that?

Esther, however, begins to get worried that Jesus seems to be foreshadowing his own death that is coming His way. He will spend three days and nights in the heart of the earth. This will be the sign that the scribes and Pharisees want before they will believe that Jesus is the long-awaited Messiah. Perhaps He is also referring to the Exodus plagues. During the ninth plague God covered all of Egypt with a thick darkness, so dark that it could be felt. Esther is sure that for all of the Egyptian common folk this sign of three days of darkness convinced them that Yahweh was the one true God. But, what will it take for the scribes and Pharisees? Will Jesus need to die and be resurrected three days later? Esther just does not know.

How about you? What kind of sign do you need to know for sure that God loves you beyond what you can imagine? Is it giant skywriting? Is it winning the lottery? Or is it just a hug and a whisper from a friend telling you that Jesus died for you?

Notes:

Matthew 12:46-50

The Family of God

46 While He was still talking to the multitudes, behold, His mother and brothers stood outside, seeking to speak with Him. 47 Then one said to Him, "Look, Your mother and Your brothers are standing outside, seeking to speak with You."

48 But He answered and said to the one who told Him, "Who is My mother and who are My brothers?" 49 And He stretched out His hand toward His disciples and said, "Here are My mother and My brothers! 50 For whoever does the will of My Father in heaven is My brother and sister and mother."

Zibeon listens to Jesus every chance he gets. Jesus is talking to the multitudes and Jesus' mother shows up. Zibeon chuckles to himself because he knows what it means when his mother shows up on the scene. Usually, it is bad news for Zibeon. Jesus' mother shows up with His four brothers and Zibeon wonders what this means. Are they here to take Jesus back to Nazareth?

Jesus answers the messenger with a question in a voice loud enough for all to hear: "Who is My mother and who are My brothers?" Zibeon thinks to himself, *They are right here in front of you, Jesus.* But Jesus seems to be thinking beyond His physical family. Jesus says that whoever does the will of His Father in heaven is His brother and sister and mother.

Wow! Zibeon is blown away. Is Jesus saying that Zibeon can be adopted into God's family as His child? He would then have full rights as a family member. Jesus has already talked about being poor in spirit, for yours is the kingdom of heaven. If Zibeon is a peacemaker, he will be called a son of God. If he does good works like being the salt of the earth or the light of the world, he will glorify his Father in heaven. These are all family messages.

Jesus seems to be really serious about the family of God, but it is not for everyone. It is only for Jesus' true followers. Zibeon is getting really excited about being adopted into God's family. He is ready to seek first the kingdom of God and His righteousness, for then all of the rights of being a family member will be his.

How about you? Are you ready to be adopted into Jesus' family? If so, can you pray this prayer?

"Lord Jesus, I need You. Thank You for dying on the cross for my sins. I open my heart and receive You as my Savior and Lord. Thank You for forgiving my sins and giving me eternal life. Please take control of the throne of my life. Make me to be the kind of person You want me to be. Amen."

If you prayed this prayer, tell a friend.

Notes:

Matthew 13:3-9

Good Soil

³ *Then He spoke many things to them in parables, saying: "Behold, a sower went out to sow. ⁴ And as he sowed, some seed fell by the wayside; and the birds came and devoured them. ⁵ Some fell on stony places, where they did not have much earth; and they immediately sprang up because they had no depth of earth. ⁶ But when the sun was up they were scorched, and because they had no root they withered away. ⁷ And some fell among thorns, and the thorns sprang up and choked them. ⁸ But others fell on good ground and yielded a crop: some a hundredfold, some sixty, some thirty. ⁹ He who has ears to hear, let him hear!"*

Jesus likes teaching with parables. He loves using everyday life stories to teach a spiritual lesson, sometimes with an interesting or surprising twist.

Philip has been a farmer all of his life. He loves working the ground. He wished he could grow more food to better provide for his family. So, he listens intently to Jesus when He talks about sowing seeds. Jesus describes the sowing process exactly like Philip does it. Philp scatters the seed throughout his field; but some seed falls outside of the field, or among the stones, or among the thorns. Most of the seed falls on the good ground and then Philp plows the seed into the soil.

Philp immediately sees that the point of the parable is that the human heart is like the ground and the seed is the word of the kingdom. Philip knows that the seed that falls outside of the field, in the wayside, never comes to anything. As it is when people hear Jesus' words and they just go in one ear and out the other.

There are always stones in Philips's field. The seed that falls among the stones sprouts up, but then quickly dies away. Just like people who hear Jesus' speak and leave happy, but the next day they have forgotten all about Jesus.

The thorny weeds are Philips's biggest nightmare because the thorny weeds always grow up with the good seed. As the thorns grow faster, they choke out the good seed. Just like the cares of the world choke out Jesus' commands for us.

The seed that falls on the good soil yields a good crop. Then Philip hears the twist: up to a hundredfold! Philip has never gotten that kind of yield on his seed. Jesus is saying that God will be so gracious that He will give blessings way beyond what we deserve.

How about you? How would you describe your heart? Is it a mix of soils? Do you need the Holy Spirit to do some earth work in your heart?

Notes:

Matthew 13:24-30

At the Harvest

24 Another parable He put forth to them, saying: "The kingdom of heaven is like a man who sowed good seed in his field; 25 but while men slept, his enemy came and sowed tares among the wheat and went his way. 26 But when the grain had sprouted and produced a crop, then the tares also appeared. 27 So the servants of the owner came and said to him, 'Sir, did you not sow good seed in your field? How then does it have tares?' 28 He said to them, 'An enemy has done this.' The servants said to him, 'Do you want us then to go and gather them up?' 29 But he said, 'No, lest while you gather up the tares you also uproot the wheat with them. 30 Let both grow together until the harvest, and at the time of harvest I will say to the reapers, "First gather together the tares and bind them in bundles to burn them, but gather the wheat into my barn."'"

Philip hears another parable from Jesus about sowing good seed. In this case, the sowing went great. The good seed went into the field. However, overnight the enemy came and sowed tares, a particularly nasty weed that looks a lot like wheat when it grows. This is a very evil act against the farmer as it could ruin his entire crop for the year. The farmer has three choices: pull everything up and start over, try to pull up just the tares knowing that some wheat will also be pulled up, or let them grow up together and separate the tares out at the time of the harvest. Philip finally agrees with the farmer in Jesus' story, let them grow together.

Philip struggles with the deeper meaning of this parable. He sees that Jesus is making several important points. One, the evil one exists and he is actively working to spoil our time here on the earth. He is making it easy for people to pretend to be Jesus' followers; they play the part, but they do not love Jesus in their hearts. Two, God allows evil to have its play on the earth. He is aware of the foiling plans of the evil one, yet He patiently withholds His judgment for the sake of the good wheat, that none would be lost. Three, there is a harvest at the end of the age. God's people will be gathered up into His barn, the kingdom of heaven. The people who do not love God will be gathered together and not only removed from God's sight, but they will be burned up.

God is serious about His kingdom of heaven because He is holy. Only pure and perfect people can come into His kingdom. How can that be, as we are all sinners? We can only be gathered into the barn if we have claimed Jesus as our Lord and Savior. If you are sure that you will be in God's kingdom at the time of the harvest because of Jesus, will you invite someone to join you? Will you tell them about Jesus?

Notes:

Matthew 13:44-46

Hidden Treasures

44 "Again, the kingdom of heaven is like treasure hidden in a field, which a man found and hid; and for joy over it he goes and sells all that he has and buys that field.

45 "Again, the kingdom of heaven is like a merchant seeking beautiful pearls, 46 who, when he had found one pearl of great price, went and sold all that he had and bought it."

Jude is listening to Jesus teach in parables. Jude understands the treasure hidden in a field analogy as he sometimes experiences this in his home building business. When he shows his customers the perfect field for their new home they run out and purchase it quickly. Jesus is giving a "so much more" analogy. In this case, it is not just a field for a house, but in the field is a hidden treasure of great value, worth so much more. In this case the man would sell everything to obtain it.

The second parable is about a merchant buying jewelry. Jude understands this as it is the perfect, final touch for a house to become a home. This is another "so much more" parable; in this case it is the one pearl of great price.

Jesus is repeating what He said earlier; "He who finds his life will lose it, and he who loses his life for My sake will find it" (Matthew 10:39). The kingdom of heaven is of exceeding great value.

Much of this time we put off pursuing the pearl of great price. We are too busy with our careers to bother with this Jesus stuff. Our family is taking all of our time. How could I possibly find time to go to church? Besides, I like to play golf on Sundays. We do not understand that Jesus is offering a new and much better life, the pearl of great price. He is offering real forgiveness. He is offering a way to deal with our guilt.

He is offering you the Holy Spirit to indwell your heart to change it and transform you into a person more like the one you were created to be. He is offering you real purpose in life. Jesus plays for keeps here; He wants you to be with Him forever.

Is it time to grab the one pearl of great price? What is it worth to you?

Notes:

Matthew 13:47-50

Dragnets to Changed Hearts

⁴⁷ "Again, the kingdom of heaven is like a dragnet that was cast into the sea and gathered some of every kind, ⁴⁸ which, when it was full, they drew to shore; and they sat down and gathered the good into vessels, but threw the bad away. ⁴⁹ So it will be at the end of the age. The angels will come forth, separate the wicked from among the just, ⁵⁰ and cast them into the furnace of fire. There will be wailing and gnashing of teeth."

Peter has been following Jesus for quite a while now. Jesus called him to be a fisher of men. Some days he feels like he is succeeding, but many days he feels like he is just trudging around the countryside. At last, Jesus is talking about fishing, something that Peter can relate to.

Jesus compares the kingdom of heaven to a dragnet. Dragnet fishing is the way Peter most commonly uses to catch lots of fish. As Jesus points out, the dragnet catches all kinds of fish. Peter has seen all kinds of people in his ministry with Jesus so far. Jews and Gentiles, young and old, tall and short, Hebrew speakers and Greek speakers. Peter knows how to identify the good fish and the bad fish and separate them, but how will God separate the wicked from the just?

Peter has learned from Jesus that it is all a matter of the heart. Jesus has been saying in many different ways that it is a matter of a changed heart. A heart that places its faith in Jesus. Peter has come to understand what faith means. It is not just intellectual assent to some idea, but it is absolute, personal trust. Just as Peter trusts that the boat will keep him afloat on the sea, Peter has come to understand that only Jesus can change his heart and make him into the man he was created to be. Peter has come to trust Jesus implicitly. But, how can one tell the wicked heart from the just heart?

Peter has heard Jesus say over and over again, our words and actions flow out of the treasure of our hearts. If we have a charged heart, our words and deeds will also be changed. Not necessarily all at once, but slowly over time they will change. Peter has seen this in his own life. His actions are more selfless now and this response is easier and more natural. He is being kinder to strangers much more often. He now can ask for forgiveness and really be forgiven. He is experiencing real joy for the first time in his life.

How about you? Are you experiencing a changed life? If not, why not?

Notes:

Matthew 14:3-9

Because of Fear

3 For Herod had laid hold of John and bound him, and put him in prison for the sake of Herodias, his brother Philip's wife. 4 Because John had said to him, "It is not lawful for you to have her." 5 And although he wanted to put him to death, he feared the multitude, because they counted him as a prophet. 6 But when Herod's birthday was celebrated, the daughter of Herodias danced before them and pleased Herod. 7 Therefore he promised with an oath to give her whatever she might ask. 8 So she, having been prompted by her mother, said, "Give me John the Baptist's head here on a platter." 9 And the king was sorry; nevertheless, because of the oaths and because of those who sat with him, he commanded it to be given to her.

Matthew is surprised to get an invitation to Herod's big birthday bash. Perhaps the invitation is in recognition of his years as a tax collector for the Romans. He is not very proud of that period of his life, but he decides to go anyway. Perhaps, he will get a chance to talk with someone about his new life with Jesus.

Herod has taken his brother's wife, Herodias as his own wife and John the Baptist has vehemently criticized Herod in public. Herod threw John in prison, but because he is afraid of the multitude, he does not kill John. Imagine that! The top Roman ruler is afraid of a bunch of dirty rabble-rousers, the Jews.

At Herod's party Herodias' daughter gives a very seductive dancing performance. Mathew is a bit embarrassed by it, but Herod and his guests love it. In front of everyone, Herod promises with an oath to give Herodias' daughter whatever she might ask for. Instead of asking for her own mansion estate or great wealth, she asks for the head of John the Baptist to be brought to her, in front of everyone.

Herod is sorry that he swore the oath in front of his guests, but because of them he must act on it or lose face; therefore, he commands it. Matthew Is very distraught because he knows and loves John, but also because Herod has acted out of fear. Herod is afraid of the multitude. Herod is afraid of what others might think of him. Herod is even afraid of his wife, Herodias. This is a horrible way for a king to act.

In contrast, Matthew thinks about Jesus as the King of kings. He does not do anything out of fear, but only out of love. He only cares to do the will of His Father. He does not care what others think of Him.

How about you? Do you do things out of fear of what others might think of you? Is it time to step out of fear and into love?

Notes:

Matthew 14:15-21

Give Them Something to Eat

15 When it was evening, His disciples came to Him, saying, "This is a deserted place, and the hour is already late. Send the multitudes away, that they may go into the villages and buy themselves food." 16 But Jesus said to them, "They do not need to go away. You give them something to eat." 17 And they said to Him, "We have here only five loaves and two fish."

18 He said, "Bring them here to Me." 19 Then He commanded the multitudes to sit down on the grass. And He took the five loaves and the two fish, and looking up to heaven, He blessed and broke and gave the loaves to the disciples; and the disciples gave to the multitudes. 20 So they all ate and were filled, and they took up twelve baskets full of the fragments that remained. 21 Now those who had eaten were about five thousand men, besides women and children.

Jesus has been teaching and healing the multitude all day. Evening is approaching. James goes to Jesus and gently tells Him that He needs to send everyone home for their evening meal; however, Jesus tells James to give them something to eat. James is flabbergasted. The disciples have already gone through the multitude looking for food, and they found only one boy with five loaves of bread and two small fish. How will that feed so many?

Jesus tells James to bring the meager food to Him and have everyone sit down as if they are getting ready for their evening meal. James is getting really, really worried here. Jesus is going to have a riot on His hands when the multitude figures out that there is not enough food for everyone.

Jesus blesses the food. James hears Jesus thanking the Father for His provision, for His lovingkindness, and for showing everyone that they do not live by bread alone. James understands that faith means trusting and James is supposed to trust Jesus and the Father to provide all of his needs, both spiritual and physical. At that moment, James takes a deep breath and simply says to himself, *I believe.*

He and the other disciples start distributing the food and there is not only enough, there is more than enough. The leftovers are more than what they started with.

James learns for the first time what "Give us this day our daily bread" means. It means to trust Jesus with all of your life: spiritual, physical, emotional, and mental. For James all of this comes from a simple statement: "You give them something to eat."

So it is with us. When Jesus tells you to "Give them something to eat," who or what will you trust?

Notes:

Matthew 14:25-33

Step Out of the Boat

25 Now in the fourth watch of the night Jesus went to them, walking on the sea. 26 And when the disciples saw Him walking on the sea, they were troubled, saying, "It is a ghost!" And they cried out for fear. 27 But immediately Jesus spoke to them, saying, "Be of good cheer! It is I; do not be afraid." 28 And Peter answered Him and said, "Lord, if it is You, command me to come to You on the water." 29 So He said, "Come." And when Peter had come down out of the boat, he walked on the water to go to Jesus. 30 But when he saw that the wind was boisterous, he was afraid; and beginning to sink he cried out, saying, "Lord, save me!" 31 And immediately Jesus stretched out His hand and caught him, and said to him, "O you of little faith, why did you doubt?" 32 And when they got into the boat, the wind ceased. 33 Then those who were in the boat came and worshiped Him, saying, "Truly You are the Son of God."

James is worn out after the miracle of the feeding of the five thousand. Jesus has sent all of the disciples in the boat to the other side of the Sea of Galilee. Unfortunately, they are going against a boisterous wind, and so the oars are out. All of a sudden, James sees a ghost walking on the sea. *Great,* he says to himself, *now I am losing my mind.*

All of a sudden Jesus hails them with "Be of good cheer!" They are all flabbergasted. Peter, always the impetuous one, calls out to Jesus and tells Him to "Command me to come to You on the water." Now James thinks that Peter has gone crazy. But he watches as Peter tentatively puts one leg over the side of the boat, and then the other. He is still holding on with both hands, and then James watches as Peter lets go with one hand and then the other. Peter is now standing on the water and then he is walking on the water towards Jesus. Walking on the water! James just cannot believe it.

James is now having a huge internal debate. *Should I step out onto the water? Will I be able to stand up? Do I need Jesus to call me? Of course not, it is just a matter of faith and trust. Do I trust that Jesus will hold me up? What about the wind and the waves? The wind is so boisterous. Is Jesus Master of this boisterous wind? Of course, but still...*

Just then, Peter becomes afraid and he begins to sink. He cries out, "Lord, save me!" James realizes that it is too late for him, he has lost his opportunity to walk on the water out to Jesus.

How about you? Where would you be with your internal debate? Can Jesus really sustain you? Do you really trust Him? Do you trust Him enough to step out of your boat?

Notes:

Matthew 15:7-11

Lips and Hearts

7 "Hypocrites! Well did Isaiah prophesy about you, saying:

8 'These people draw near to Me with their mouth,
And honor Me with their lips,
But their heart is far from Me.
9 And in vain they worship Me,
Teaching as doctrines the commandments of men.'"

10 When He had called the multitude to Himself, He said to them, "Hear and understand: 11 Not what goes into the mouth defiles a man; but what comes out of the mouth, this defiles a man."

Some of the scribes and Pharisees made the multi-day journey from Jerusalem to Galilee to check out this new rabbi, Jesus. They have been talking with Jesus about ritual hand washing before eating and staying away from Gentiles, for Jesus does neither of these things.

Jesus rails at them and calls them hypocrites, play actors. He references a prophecy from Isaiah when he talks about people honoring God with their lips, while their hearts are far from Him. This is one of Jesus' key messages: it is all about a changed heart. God is not impressed with people who go through the motions of worship if their worship does not come from their heart. After all, the most important act of worship is to love the Lord your God with all your heart, with all your soul, and with all your strength. The scribes and Pharisees love performing the act of worship much more than they love God.

Jesus expands on His message with the multitude, explaining that it is not impure washing or eating which defiles us. If the love of God is not treasured in our hearts, what comes out of our mouths shows our defilement.

It is the same today. Yes, corporate worship is important to our spiritual growth. It is a time to be a part of a community of believers. It is a place to receive Holy Communion. It is a joy to worship with others in song and prayer. But, it does us no good if we are just going through the motions and our hearts are far away.

The next time you go to worship, remember you are in the presence of a holy God and He requires that you love Him with your entire being, your heart and mind and emotions. When you leave worship, go to love and serve the Lord. Will you do these things the next time you attend a worship service?

Notes:

Matthew 15:21-28

Mercy, Undeserved Grace

21 Then Jesus went out from there and departed to the region of Tyre and Sidon. 22 And behold, a woman of Canaan came from that region and cried out to Him, saying, "Have mercy on me, O Lord, Son of David! My daughter is severely demon-possessed." 23 But He answered her not a word. And His disciples came and urged Him, saying, "Send her away, for she cries out after us." 24 But He answered and said, "I was not sent except to the lost sheep of the house of Israel." 25 Then she came and worshiped Him, saying, "Lord, help me!" 26 But He answered and said, "It is not good to take the children's bread and throw it to the little dogs." 27 And she said, "Yes, Lord, yet even the little dogs eat the crumbs which fall from their masters' table." 28 Then Jesus answered and said to her, "O woman, great is your faith! Let it be to you as you desire." And her daughter was healed from that very hour.

Abigail is in the western region of Tyre when Jesus comes traveling through. A Canaanite woman stops Him in the street. Abigail thinks that this is very strange because the Canaanite woman is far from home and she is a pagan, not a Jew. Abigail immediately identifies with her, because she is crying out for her daughter.

111

Jesus seems to be in a hurry because He does not acknowledge her. He is on a mission. She keeps crying out to Jesus and the disciples are becoming embarrassed. Jesus explains that His mission, now, is to the Jews, the house of Israel.

However, the Canaanite woman is not to be thwarted, so she stops Jesus, worships Him and then cries out with the simplest and most powerful prayer: "Lord, help me!" Again, Jesus responds strangely and calls her a little dog. At this time, household pets were typically small, well-trained dogs, referred to as "little dogs." The larger, feral dogs that roamed the streets, feeding on garbage, were not called little dogs.

She acknowledges Jesus' comment about her and she responds that yes, she is a household dog. She is not a child of the house of Israel. She deserves nothing from Jesus. She is entitled to nothing from Him; yet she asks for undeserved mercy. Jesus is surprised by her great faith. He is pleased that she realizes what mercy is, undeserved grace. Abigail wonders why more Jews cannot understand this idea of undeserved grace.

Jesus would be pleased if more of us understood mercy, undeserved grace. So often in our prayers, we pray like God owes us His goodness and mercy. Mercy is never owed; it is always undeserved. Will you thank Him today for His undeserved grace which He has poured out on you?

Notes:

Matthew 16:13-17

Who Do You Say That I Am?

13 When Jesus came into the region of Caesarea Philippi, He asked His disciples, saying, "Who do men say that I, the Son of Man, am?"

14 So they said, "Some say John the Baptist, some Elijah, and others Jeremiah or one of the prophets."

15 He said to them, "But who do you say that I am?"

16 Simon Peter answered and said, "You are the Christ, the Son of the living God."

17 Jesus answered and said to him, "Blessed are you, Simon Bar-Jonah, for flesh and blood has not revealed this to you, but My Father who is in heaven..."

Jesus is having a quiet evening with His disciples and He asks for a public opinion poll. He wants to know who everyone thinks He is. There are huge theological debates running among the religious leaders – the Pharisees – about whether the Messiah will come as the new high priest. Some of the common folk think that the Messiah will come as the new king and He will overthrow the Roman rulers. The scribes think that Elijah has to come before the Messiah, so perhaps Jesus is the resurrected Elijah or some other prophet.

Jesus turns the discussion to the disciples. Matthew is sorry for all those years that he worked as a tax collector for the Roman rulers. He has come to hate his Roman bosses. He would be happy if Jesus would kick them out of Israel, but he cannot see how Jesus can do that. James knows enough to know that some hoped that John the Baptist was Elijah, but it was not so. Perhaps Jesus really is Elijah.

"But, who do you say that I am?" They have all been living day in and day out with Jesus for many months. They should know who He is, this should be simple; and yet it is not. Finally, Peter says: "You are the Christ, the Son of the living God."

So, how about you? What do you say? After being with Jesus for a while, it is obvious that you only have two options. Many say that He was just a good teacher, a good moralist. Unfortunately, the problem with that answer is that He called Himself Immanuel, God with us. So, if this is not true, He is not God and He is a crazy man and therefore He cannot be a good teacher. He has to be either a crazy man like many after Him who claimed to be God, or He really is the Christ, the Son of the living God. There are only two possible answers to the question. It is your turn; how do you answer Jesus when He asks you "Who do you say that I am?"

Notes:

Matthew 16:21-26

Save Yourself?

21 From that time Jesus began to show to His disciples that He must go to Jerusalem, and suffer many things from the elders and chief priests and scribes, and be killed, and be raised the third day.

22 Then Peter took Him aside and began to rebuke Him, saying, "Far be it from You, Lord; this shall not happen to You!" 23 But He turned and said to Peter, "Get behind Me, Satan! You are an offense to Me, for you are not mindful of the things of God, but the things of men."

24 Then Jesus said to His disciples, "If anyone desires to come after Me, let him deny himself, and take up his cross, and follow Me. 25 For whoever desires to save his life will lose it, but whoever loses his life for My sake will find it. 26 For what profit is it to a man if he gains the whole world, and loses his own soul? Or what will a man give in exchange for his soul..."

Jesus is going go to Jerusalem. He is the only One who truly understands what this means. He is the only One who was born to die, specifically to die to pay the penalty for all of the sins committed by God's people who claim Him as their Lord and

Savior. Peter, like us, does not understand this. With a typical arrogant human reaction, Peter rebukes the Lord of the Universe.

Jesus sees Peter's rebuke for what it is, a direct attack by Satan. This is just like Satan's original attacks in the wilderness, trying to get Jesus to take the easy path. When Satan failed there "he departed from Him until an opportune time" (Luke 4:13).

Jesus then follows this with a clear message for us. If we want to receive the gift of Jesus' death on the cross, we need to claim Him not just as our Savior, but also as our Lord. If He is Lord, we must deny ourselves. We must give up our own self-centered view of life and we must submit to His authority.

If we are to come after Him, we must lose our lives. We must give up control to Him. Only when we do this will we save our lives, will we become who we were created to be. Jesus promises us so much. He promises to be the light for our path. He promises to sustain us in body and soul with His bread. He promises to be our shepherd and keep us from wandering aimlessly in this world. He promises us forgiveness and He promises to remove our guilt as far as the east is from the west. He promises that His Spirit will indwell us forever.

He promises to be with you always, even to the end of the age. Yes, it is hard to deny yourself and lose your life; but that is the only way to save your life. Are you ready?

Notes:

Matthew 17:1-5

Hear Him!

¹ Now after six days Jesus took Peter, James, and John his brother, led them up on a high mountain by themselves; ² and He was transfigured before them. His face shone like the sun, and His clothes became as white as the light. ³ And behold, Moses and Elijah appeared to them, talking with Him. ⁴ Then Peter answered and said to Jesus, "Lord, it is good for us to be here; if You wish, let us make here three tabernacles: one for You, one for Moses, and one for Elijah."

⁵ While he was still speaking, behold, a bright cloud overshadowed them; and suddenly a voice came out of the cloud, saying, "This is My beloved Son, in whom I am well pleased. Hear Him!"

It was not very often that Jesus went off with just a few of us, but this was one of those times. Jesus asked Peter, my brother John, and me to go up to a high mountain. I had no idea what this was about; I was thinking that it was to be a special time of prayer, as Jesus would often go away to talk to His Father.

When we got to the top of the mountain, it began with Jesus talking with His Father. All of a sudden, Jesus' face was totally transfigured. It was shining like the sun, but from the inside. It was not a reflected light. It was His own light. He was so bright that His clothes also became as white as the light.

All of a sudden, out of nowhere, I saw Moses and Elijah appear. I knew who they were, as if the Holy Spirit was speaking directly to my heart and mind. I saw Moses, Elijah, and Jesus having a conversation. If I understood it right, they were discussing what was about to happen in Jerusalem. Moses and Elijah seemed to be reminding Jesus of all that they had foretold in the past.

Then Peter came out of his stupor and said that we should build three tents so that this could go on forever. It was so beautiful; I wanted the same thing. Then out of a bright cloud, the voice of God the Father said: "This is My beloved Son, in whom I am well pleased. Hear Him!" I fell on my face for I do not know how long, and worshiped God and His beloved Son. The next thing I knew, Jesus was Himself again, He tapped me on the shoulder and told me to get up and to not be afraid.

I will never forget that time on the mountain. I saw the glorified Christ. I heard God the Father. I felt the Holy Spirit touch my heart. If you have never had an experience like this, you can share mine with me. Can you remember that the Father said, "Hear Him!" and that Jesus said to not be afraid?

Notes:

Matthew 17:24-27

Cast Your Line

24 When they had come to Capernaum, those who received the temple tax came to Peter and said, "Does your Teacher not pay the temple tax?"

25 He said, "Yes."

And when he had come into the house, Jesus anticipated him, saying, "What do you think, Simon? From whom do the kings of the earth take customs or taxes, from their sons or from strangers?"

26 Peter said to Him, "From strangers."

Jesus said to him, "Then the sons are free. 27 Nevertheless, lest we offend them, go to the sea, cast in a hook, and take the fish that comes up first. And when you have opened its mouth, you will find a piece of money; take that and give it to them for Me and you."

Jesus is nearing the end of His time in Galilee. He and his disciples are staying in Capernaum near the Sea of Galilee. Peter is approached by some of the rulers of the local synagogue and he is asked if Jesus pays the temple tax. The temple tax was originally instituted by Moses during the building of the tabernacle. It was to be a one-time tax, the same amount for every man. Later, the priests made it into an annual tax. The rulers are trying to trick Jesus again, but Peter says that they will pay the temple tax.

Jesus then asks Peter a strange question about kings and their taxation. Do kings tax their own family members? No, generally not. Only the non-family members, strangers, are taxed. Jesus then says that He should not have to pay the temple tax. God is the King of the temple, and, as His Son, Jesus is exempt from the temple tax. Jesus is again declaring to all around that He is the Son of God.

Even though He is exempt from the temple tax, He agrees that they will pay it. Jesus decides that another visual sign is needed to clarify that He is indeed the Son of God. He tells Peter to go out onto the Sea of Galilee and cast a hook, just once.

Peter is really sweating this situation. He must be thinking, *Where is the right spot to row to? What kind of bait am I supposed to use? What happens if I don't cast the line right? Do I get a do-over?* Nonetheless, Peter does as Jesus commands and, lo and behold, the first fish caught has a coin in his mouth. Peter is blown away by this miracle. Again, this is exactly what is needed.

Jesus will sometimes give us seemingly strange tasks to do. However, they will always be the right things to do. When He gives you one of these, will you just row out and cast your line?

Notes:

Matthew 18:1-5

Become as Little Children

¹ At that time the disciples came to Jesus, saying, "Who then is greatest in the kingdom of heaven?"

² Then Jesus called a little child to Him, set him in the midst of them, ³ and said, "Assuredly, I say to you, unless you are converted and become as little children, you will by no means enter the kingdom of heaven. ⁴ Therefore whoever humbles himself as this little child is the greatest in the kingdom of heaven. ⁵ Whoever receives one little child like this in My name receives Me."

The disciples are arguing among themselves about who is the greatest in the kingdom of heaven. Is it someone of old, like Moses or Elijah; or is it John the Baptist; or is it one of them, like Peter? After all, they have been traveling with Jesus for several years now, maybe it is one of them? Sarah is in the crowd with her little old brother. To Sarah's surprise, Jesus calls her over to Him. He takes her little brother and uses him as His example and says, "Unless you are converted and become as little children, you will by no means enter the kingdom of heaven."

Sarah is very surprised by this. She knows her brother is a good boy most of time, but at times he is a real brat, a little dictator. He demands things and then cries when he does not get them. However, Sarah sees implicit trust, implicit faith in him. Whenever he is afraid to do something and his mother tells him that it will be okay and then reaches out her hand, her brother takes the hand and moves forward with total trust.

Sarah immediately understands that the adults arguing about who is the greatest are definitely not humble like a child. They are only thinking about how great they are. Sarah does not see them implicitly trusting Jesus, she sees them arguing with Him and each other. Sarah has seen that adults argue a lot and seem to lose their sense of joy, their imaginations, and their trust in others. Why is that?

Sarah swears to herself that she will not lose her joy, her imagination, or her trust in Jesus as she gets older. How about you? Do you need to get back in touch with your trusting inner child? Do you need to take His hand?

Notes:

Matthew 18:11-12

Lost Sheep

11 For the Son of Man has come to save that which was lost.

12 "What do you think? If a man has a hundred sheep, and one of them goes astray, does he not leave the ninety-nine and go to the mountains to seek the one that is straying? 13 And if he should find it, assuredly, I say to you, he rejoices more over that sheep than over the ninety-nine that did not go astray."

As Jesus is walking through the countryside with his disciples, He sees a flock of sheep grazing in the meadow with their shepherd nearby. Jesus uses this as a time to explain to Matthew (the tax collector) and the other disciples something about caring for the sheep.

Jesus tells Matthew that the shepherd allows the hundred sheep to freely graze in the meadow but he is always keeping an eye on them. He counts them several times a day to make sure that they are all present and accounted for. The shepherd knows that the sheep can easily get distracted and wander astray. If after his count he comes up short, he counts again. If he still comes up short, he must go to find the lost sheep before it comes to harm.

He will leave the ninety-nine with another shepherd, or a hired hand, or lock them in a sheep pen so that they will be safe and he can go seek the one that has strayed away. Sometimes the shepherd will be gone for quite some time before he finds the lost sheep. When he finally finds the lost sheep, he rejoices and then takes the lost sheep with him, back home.

Matthew knows from the history of King David that he was once a shepherd. He had to convince King Saul that he was worthy to fight Goliath, so he described his time defending his flock of sheep: "When a lion or a bear came and took a lamb out of the flock, I went out after it and struck it, and delivered the lamb from its mouth; and when it arose against me, I caught it by its beard, and struck and killed it" (I Samuel 17:34b-35). Not only did David know how to go after the one lost sheep, but he also knew how to protect the entire flock. Matthew realizes that this is why Jesus calls Himself the good shepherd. He perfectly knows how to take care of His entire flock, how to protect them from the attacks of the evil one. He also perfectly knows how to bring each of us individually back when we have gone astray.

If you think that you have gone astray and you are lost, will you lift up your head and look for the good shepherd coming your way?

Notes:

Matthew 18:15-17

Go and Talk to Him

15 "Moreover if your brother sins against you, go and tell him his fault between you and him alone. If he hears you, you have gained your brother. 16 But if he will not hear, take with you one or two more, that 'by the mouth of two or three witnesses every word may be established.' 17 And if he refuses to hear them, tell it to the church. But if he refuses even to hear the church, let him be to you like a heathen and a tax collector."

Eli is telling his son about a time when he got to listen in on one of Jesus' teachings about getting along with fellow believers. Eli remembers this as a great time, as it changed his life.

"I was always angry with people, including fellow believers, my brothers in the faith. I hated it, but I did not know what to do about it. My biggest problem back then was that I used back-biting and gossip as one of my chief weapons. If I was angry at someone for what he did to me, I would go behind his back and spread exaggerated tales about him. To no one's surprise, it did not make the situation any better, it just made everyone angrier.

"Then I heard Jesus' teaching. He said that if a brother has sinned against me, the very first thing for me to do was to go and talk to him. Jesus said I was to tell him his fault, in a calm and gentle voice, to see if we could get to the root of the problem. After I started doing this, I was surprised at how well it worked. We would talk about the problem, clear the air and at the end, I gained my brother back. It was wonderful.

"However, it did not always work, so Jesus said to try again; but this time take one or two brothers with me. Typically, they were not personally involved in the situation and could bring real wisdom from seeing both sides of the situation. When my brother and I were reconciled by this process, it brought me great joy. It felt so much better than being an angry gossip.

"However, just once, the brother would not hear the wisdom from the three of us, so we brought the problem before the entire church. Boy, I remember being really frightened in this situation. He still would not budge, so the entire church followed Jesus' teaching and put him out of the fellowship until he was ready to repent. Now in hindsight, I don't know why it took me so long to learn this lesson: 'Go and talk to him.'"

Do you have a problem or a dispute with a brother or sister? If so, will you go and talk to them? Will you ask the Holy Spirit to bring wisdom to the situation?

Notes:

Matthew 18:23-33

Forgive Him the Debt

23 *"Therefore the kingdom of heaven is like a certain king who wanted to settle accounts with his servants.* 24 *And when he had begun to settle accounts, one was brought to him who owed him ten thousand talents.* 25 *But as he was not able to pay, his master commanded that he be sold, with his wife and children and all that he had, and that payment be made.* 26 *The servant therefore fell down before him, saying, 'Master, have patience with me, and I will pay you all.'* 27 *Then the master of that servant was moved with compassion, released him, and forgave him the debt.*

28 *"But that servant went out and found one of his fellow servants who owed him a hundred denarii; and he laid hands on him and took him by the throat, saying, 'Pay me what you owe!'* 29 *So his fellow servant fell down at his feet and begged him, saying, 'Have patience with me, and I will pay you all.'* 30 *And he would not, but went and threw him into prison till he should pay the debt.* 31 *So when his fellow servants saw what had been done, they were very grieved, and came and told their master all that had been done.* 32 *Then his master, after he had called him,*

said to him, 'You wicked servant! I forgave you all that debt because you begged me. [33] Should you not also have had compassion on your fellow servant, just as I had pity on you?'"

Jesus gives another illustration on forgiveness, this time using debts. In this illustration, one of the king's servants owed the king ten thousand talents. As a denarius was the daily wage, and a talent was equivalent to six thousand denarii, this debt was an enormous debt. Matthew knew of some Jews who owed some tax debts, but nothing like this. The master commanded that the debtor be sold into slavery to help pay for his debt, as was common in the day. The servant begged for mercy and the master was moved with compassion and so he forgave the entire, enormous debt. Matthew could not believe this. He had forgiven a few small tax debts in his day, but nothing even close to a debt of this size. Matthew realizes that this servant must have been exceedingly grateful.

However, a second servant owed the forgiven debtor a hundred denarii and the original debtor would not forgive him. Matthew could not believe this, but then he suddenly sees the point of this illustration. Jesus has forgiven Matthew of a huge debt to God for all of the sins that he has committed. Yet, does Matthew freely forgive others?

We are to live as forgiven debtors who freely forgive others. How are you doing at forgiving?

Notes:

Matthew 19:16-22

How May I Have Eternal Life?

16 Now behold, one came and said to Him, "Good Teacher, what good thing shall I do that I may have eternal life?" 17 So He said to him, "Why do you call Me good? No one is good but One, that is, God. But if you want to enter into life, keep the commandments." 18 He said to Him, "Which ones?" Jesus said, "'You shall not murder,' 'You shall not commit adultery,' 'You shall not steal,' 'You shall not bear false witness,' 19 'Honor your father and your mother,' and, 'You shall love your neighbor as yourself.' " 20 The young man said to Him, "All these things I have kept from my youth. What do I still lack?" 21 Jesus said to him, "If you want to be perfect, go, sell what you have and give to the poor, and you will have treasure in heaven; and come, follow Me." 22 But when the young man heard that saying, he went away sorrowful, for he had great possessions.

A certain, young, wealthy man came to Jesus and asked Him what good thing he needs to do to ensure that he may have eternal life. In a typical rabbinical fashion, Jesus answered the questions with a question: "Why do you call Me good? No one is good but One, that is, God." Jesus is setting the stage for goodness. Jesus is making it clear that to have eternal life, you must meet God's standard of goodness, which is Himself.

Jesus clarified goodness further by using the second part of the Ten Commandments, and then summarized with: "You shall love your neighbor as yourself." Isaac has been listening to this theological exchange and he thinks to himself, *This ruler is in trouble now. No one has kept those commandments even for one day.* So, Isaac is very surprised when the young man says that he has kept all of those commandments every day since his youth.

Jesus saw into the young man's heart and knew that he had not kept those commandments for even one day. Therefore, Jesus kindly switched to the first commandment: "You shall have no other gods before Me." Isaac sees that the young man was struck to the heart. He loved his possessions. He could not possibly give up those possessions because he loved them greatly, more than God.

Isaac sees that Jesus is focused on the state of the heart. In one sense, it is easy to have eternal life, we just need to place all of our possessions, talents, and desires at the foot of God's throne for Him to have and use. After all, God owns all of these things anyway. But Isaac thought, *Can I do this?*

How about you? Can you place all of your possessions, talents, and desires at the foot of God's Throne?

Notes:

Matthew 20:1-2, 6-14

Eleventh Hour

¹"For the kingdom of heaven is like a landowner who went out early in the morning to hire laborers for his vineyard. ² Now when he had agreed with the laborers for a denarius a day, he sent them into his vineyard.

⁶ "And about the eleventh hour he went out and found others standing idle, and said to them, 'Why have you been standing here idle all day?' ⁷ They said to him, 'Because no one hired us.' He said to them, 'You also go into the vineyard, and whatever is right you will receive.' ⁸ "So when evening had come, the owner of the vineyard said to his steward, 'Call the laborers and give them their wages, beginning with the last to the first.' ⁹ And when those came who were hired about the eleventh hour, they each received a denarius. ¹⁰ But when the first came, they supposed that they would receive more; and they likewise received each a denarius. ¹¹ And when they had received it, they complained against the landowner, ¹² saying, 'These last men have worked only one hour, and you made them equal to us who have borne the burden and the heat of the day.' ¹³ But he answered one of them and said, 'Friend, I am doing you no wrong. Did you not agree with me for a denarius? 14 Take what is yours and go your way. I wish to give to this last man the same as to you.'"

Jesus tells a very simple, everyday story about justice and mercy. Jude often works with other home builders as a hired hand. As a daily laborer, he tries try to start early in the day so that he can make the most money. Sometimes other workers start later in the day and Jude knows that they will be making less than the denarius as that is the fair and just wage.

However, in this story, the last men who started at the eleventh hour of the day also received a denarius. Jude wants to scream, "That's not fair!" Jesus is making the point that those who worked the entire day received their just and fair wages. With those who started at the eleventh hour there was no injustice, there was just mercy. Mercy is never owed; it is freely given. Jude sees the point of the story. He received what he was owed. He got justice. Those who started at the eleventh hour did not get injustice, they got mercy. Jude knows that if he starts the next day at the eleventh hour, he should not expect mercy. Mercy can never be expected, it can only be joyously received.

Jude came to see that as a sinner he does not want justice from God, as the punishment would be severe. He only wants the free gift that comes through the sacrifice of Jesus. How about you? Do you want justice or mercy?

Notes:

Matthew 20:17-19

Will Be Betrayed

17 Now Jesus, going up to Jerusalem, took the twelve disciples aside on the road and said to them, 18 "Behold, we are going up to Jerusalem, and the Son of Man will be betrayed to the chief priests and to the scribes; and they will condemn Him to death, 19 and deliver Him to the Gentiles to mock and to scourge and to crucify. And the third day He will rise again."

Jesus has spent much of His ministry in the northern region of Galilee. He is now headed south to go to Jerusalem, the religious center of Israel. As He is walking, He tells His twelve disciples that He will be betrayed.

He talks about the horrible things that will happen to Him; He will be condemned to death, mocked, scourged, and crucified. Oddly, James gets stuck on the word betrayed. Betrayal is one of the most devastating losses a person can experience. It is a total loss of trust, love, and friendship in a close personal relationship.

James remembers the time that he was betrayed. He and one of his very close friends were going to form a new business. They were going to transform the fishing business off of the Sea of Galilee. They were going to change the way the fish were brought to market. It was a brilliant plan. And then, his friend and "partner" went and carried out the business plan with one of James' competitors and enemies. Afterwards, James kept thinking over and over, *How could he do this to me? Why did he break our trust, our friendship? Didn't he say that he would be by my side forever? Did I do something wrong?*

James knows that he did not do anything wrong. He did not instigate the betrayal. It all came from the other person's heart. James begins to wonder if he has ever betrayed anyone's trust and love like this.

So it is with us. We betray God's lovingkindness every day. He tells us of His love for us. He blesses us beyond what we deserve. He tells us how we are to engage with those around us. We tell God that we love Him and that we will love others and then… we betray Him. We go our own way and do not act like we love Him the way we say that we do. We are betrayers.

Will you repent of your betrayal today?

Notes:

Matthew 20:20-21, 24-28

Servant Leader

20 Then the mother of Zebedee's sons came to Him with her sons, kneeling down and asking something from Him. 21 And He said to her, "What do you wish?" She said to Him, "Grant that these two sons of mine may sit, one on Your right hand and the other on the left, in Your kingdom."

24 And when the ten heard it, they were greatly displeased with the two brothers. 25 But Jesus called them to Himself and said, "You know that the rulers of the Gentiles lord it over them, and those who are great exercise authority over them. 26 Yet it shall not be so among you; but whoever desires to become great among you, let him be your servant. 27 And whoever desires to be first among you, let him be your slave— 28 just as the Son of Man did not come to be served, but to serve, and to give His life a ransom for many."

James is surprised to see his mother come to speak to Jesus. At first, he thinks that she is bringing some home-cooked food or an offering from the local synagogue; but then he hears his mother asking Jesus if he and his brother John might sit in the most favored positions in Jesus' kingdom, on the right and on the left.

James feels a wide range of emotions: pride that his mother would ask this, embarrassment that his mother would ask this, and then he thinks, *Would I be on the right hand?* He then looks at the other disciples and he is deeply distraught. They are greatly displeased. He knows what they must be thinking, *What makes you so special that you would be great among us, that you would be first?*

Jesus steps in to defuse the swelling anger. He reminds them of what they hate about the Roman rulers: how they lord their authority over the Jewish people. Jesus tells them that it shall not be so for them. Jesus tells them if they want to be great, they must be a servant or a slave. Jesus gives them two different words to get the point across. In some cases, they are to be an attendant, like a waiter at table, or a foot-washing servant at the door. In other cases, they are to be a bondservant, a person who intentionally places himself as a servant to a master, letting the master be in charge.

We sometimes hear this language today, the idea of being a "servant leader." However, many times these are just idle words. We don't really want to be the servant of those poor, ignorant sheep who need a real leader like us. But Jesus is serious about this. He wants us to be real foot washers, and expect no praise or glory from doing the lowly jobs. Will you turn your heart today to serve someone else without expecting any reward or praise?

Notes:

Matthew 20:29-34

And They Followed Him

29 Now as they went out of Jericho, a great multitude followed Him. 30 And behold, two blind men sitting by the road, when they heard that Jesus was passing by, cried out, saying, "Have mercy on us, O Lord, Son of David!"

31 Then the multitude warned them that they should be quiet; but they cried out all the more, saying, "Have mercy on us, O Lord, Son of David!"

32 So Jesus stood still and called them, and said, "What do you want Me to do for you?"

33 They said to Him, "Lord, that our eyes may be opened." 34 So Jesus had compassion and touched their eyes. And immediately their eyes received sight, and they followed Him.

Two blind men are waiting for Jesus as He leaves Jericho. The multitude hear them cry out to Jesus for His mercy. They try to make the two blind men shush up, but they cry out all the more. From the noise of the multitude's movement, the blind men realize that they have gotten Jesus' attention. He calls to them and asks a curious question: "What do you want Me to do for you?"

They could have asked for a lot of things. They could have asked for great wealth. They could have asked for a large mansion filled with servants. They could have asked for a long life. However, they ask for the most obvious thing, that their eyes may be opened. Jesus reaches out in compassion and touches their eyes and immediately they receive their sight. Once they receive their sight, they follow Him.

Often, we do not know what to ask God for. In our prayers we ask for many good things: for healing, for financial security, for reconciliation with a friend or family member. Jesus knows that these are all good things; however, they are not the best. They are not what we truly need. Jesus wants to open the eyes of our hearts so that we may know Him. He wants us to know our calling, the riches of the glory of His inheritance (Ephesians 1:18). He wants nothing more than for us to get up and follow Him.

How about you? What does Jesus want you to ask for? What will be the biggest thing, wish, or desire that will help you to want to rise up and see Him more clearly, to love Him more dearly, and to follow Him more nearly?

Notes:

Matthew 21:1-9 (Part 1)

The King Comes

¹ Now when they drew near Jerusalem, and came to Bethphage, at the Mount of Olives, then Jesus sent two disciples, ² saying to them, "Go into the village opposite you, and immediately you will find a donkey tied, and a colt with her. Loose them and bring them to Me. ³ And if anyone says anything to you, you shall say, 'The Lord has need of them,' and immediately he will send them."

⁴ All this was done that it might be fulfilled which was spoken by the prophet, saying:

⁵ "Tell the daughter of Zion,
'Behold, your King is coming to you,
Lowly, and sitting on a donkey,
A colt, the foal of a donkey.'"

⁶ So the disciples went and did as Jesus commanded them. ⁷ They brought the donkey and the colt, laid their clothes on them, and set Him on them. ⁸ And a very great multitude spread their clothes on the road; others cut down branches from the trees and spread them on the road. ⁹ Then the multitudes who went before and those who followed cried out, saying:

"Hosanna to the Son of David!
'Blessed is He who comes in the name of the
*   LORD!'*
Hosanna in the highest!"

Jesus is finally coming into Jerusalem, the religious center of Israel. The disciples have been waiting for this moment for almost three years. They are thinking that this is going to be a great event: *The Messiah will ride into the city on a large, white stallion and He will kick out both the Roman and the religious rules. He will set Himself up as King on a throne that lasts forever.*

The first surprise is that He sends two disciples to get a young donkey. Why is He getting a donkey instead of a stallion? Jesus reminds them that He is fulfilling an ancient prophecy made by Zechariah five hundred years before.

The multitude is not going to have its enthusiasm dampened; the people spread their clothes and tree branches on the road and cry out, "Blessed is he who comes in the name of the LORD! We have blessed you from the house of the LORD" (Psalm 118:26).

The multitude got this right. Greatly to be praised is the Messiah as he comes to save His people. Will you join in with the multitude and bless the Lord?

Notes:

Matthew 21:1-9 (Part 2)

The Suffering Servant Comes

¹ Now when they drew near Jerusalem, and came to Bethphage, at the Mount of Olives, then Jesus sent two disciples, ² saying to them, "Go into the village opposite you, and immediately you will find a donkey tied, and a colt with her. Loose them and bring them to Me. ³ And if anyone says anything to you, you shall say, 'The Lord has need of them,' and immediately he will send them."

⁴ All this was done that it might be fulfilled which was spoken by the prophet, saying:

⁵ "Tell the daughter of Zion,
'Behold, your King is coming to you,
Lowly, and sitting on a donkey,
A colt, the foal of a donkey.'"

⁶ So the disciples went and did as Jesus commanded them. ⁷ They brought the donkey and the colt, laid their clothes on them, and set Him on them. ⁸ And a very great multitude spread their clothes on the road; others cut down branches from the trees and spread them on the road. ⁹ Then the multitudes who went before and those who followed cried out, saying:

"Hosanna to the Son of David!

'Blessed is He who comes in the name of the
    L*ORD!'*
Hosanna in the highest!"

Jesus is totally destroying everyone's expectation as to who the Messiah would be and what He would do. He is not coming to kick out the Roman rulers. He is not coming to challenge the religious leaders. He is not going to solve everyone's problems or heal everyone. He has come for a different reason. "Surely He has borne our griefs and carried our sorrows; Yet we esteemed Him stricken, smitten by God, and afflicted. But He was wounded for our transgressions, He was bruised for our iniquities; The chastisement for our peace was upon Him, and by His stripes we are healed" (Isaiah 53:4-5).

Only after He has been the suffering Servant and been crucified and buried will He rise from the dead and take His rightful place in the kingdom of God. He will then reign forever; He will provide a way for God's people to claim His robe of righteousness to cover their sins. Only then will He accept the praise of "Hosanna in the highest."

This is how we start our personal relationship with Jesus: we accept His sacrifice as a payment for the penalty of our sins. Only after that can we see Him as King of kings and Lord of lords. Will you worship Jesus as the suffering Servant, Messiah today?

Notes:

Matthew 21:12-13

House of Prayer

12 Then Jesus went into the temple of God and drove out all those who bought and sold in the temple, and overturned the tables of the money changers and the seats of those who sold doves. 13 And He said to them, "It is written, 'My house shall be called a house of prayer,' but you have made it a 'den of thieves.'"

Jesus goes into the temple in Jerusalem and He is very displeased, on several levels.

First, He sees a grand display of religion, religion being man's attempt to reach up to God and create God in man's own image. The religious leaders at that time had made all kinds of religious rules that had nothing to do with loving God or your neighbor. God had instituted the animal sacrifice system as a way of being aware of personal sin and asking for forgiveness. However, the temple leaders had added a few more layers of religiosity. Many poor worshipers who came from a long way away could not bring their sacrifice animals with them, so the temple officials set up a marketplace on the temple grounds to sell animals for sacrifice. The only way to buy these animals was with temple coins. Of course, none of the people had temple coins, so they needed to exchange their own money for temple coins. The money changers would often cheat on the exchange rate and then pocket the difference.

Second, the temple was supposed to be a place of worship and prayer. The selling of the animals and exchanging of money made it a very loud place. It was not conducive to prayer. Jesus reminds them of Jeremiah's words about right living and right worship (Jeremiah 7:5-11).

Third, the outer court, where all of this selling was taking place, was to be a safe place where Gentiles could visit the temple. They could witness Jews in worship and they could discuss the worship of God with the Jews. The Jews could even pray for their Gentile neighbors who came to visit the outer court.

Do we still do this today? Is our worship all about being religious, thinking that by doing certain things we will make God happy so that we can earn His blessing and salvation? Do we invite unbelievers to worship with us; do we pray with them? What can you do today to make your place of worship a place where God is truly worshiped?

Notes:

Matthew 21:23-27

By What Authority?

23 Now when He came into the temple, the chief priests and the elders of the people confronted Him as He was teaching, and said, "By what authority are You doing these things? And who gave You this authority?"

24 But Jesus answered and said to them, "I also will ask you one thing, which if you tell Me, I likewise will tell you by what authority I do these things: 25 The baptism of John— where was it from? From heaven or from men?"

And they reasoned among themselves, saying, "If we say, 'From heaven,' He will say to us, 'Why then did you not believe him?' 26 But if we say, 'From men,' we fear the multitude, for all count John as a prophet." 27 So they answered Jesus and said, "We do not know."

And He said to them, "Neither will I tell you by what authority I do these things."

Jesus is in the temple when the chief priests and elders confront Him. They wanted to know, "Just Who do You think You are?" Their question is all about authority. In true rabbinical fashion, Jesus answers their question with a question. "The baptism of John—where was it from? From heaven or from men?"

145

The religious leaders realize that they are in a bind. If John baptized with God's authority, why didn't they believe him? The multitude believed John was a true prophet of God, so the religious leaders do not want to go against popular opinion. Therefore, the religious leaders cop out and do not answer Jesus.

Isaac is nearby and hears this dialogue with the religion leaders. He is very disappointed. He knows that many of the religious leaders have seen the miraculous healing signs that Jesus has done. They all know that miracles are signs to point to God and His authority. They all know that Jesus must come from God, with His authority, for no one could do these signs unless God was with Him.

For many of us, authority is the key issue. We know in our heads that God exists. We know that He has created a wonderful world. We know that He has given us laws to live by. We know that these laws are good and good for us. That part of God is all good. However, the idea of Him having authority over our lives, being our Master, that is hard for some of us to swallow. As Jesus said earlier, if you want real and abundant life, you must give control of your life to Him, you must lose yourself to His authority. Will you once again, or for the first time, submit to His authority?

Notes:

Matthew 21:28-32

Reluctant Obedience

²⁸ "But what do you think? A man had two sons, and he came to the first and said, 'Son, go, work today in my vineyard.' ²⁹ He answered and said, 'I will not,' but afterward he regretted it and went. ³⁰ Then he came to the second and said likewise. And he answered and said, 'I go, sir,' but he did not go. ³¹ Which of the two did the will of his father?"

They said to Him, "The first."

Jesus said to them, "Assuredly, I say to you that tax collectors and harlots enter the kingdom of God before you. ³² For John came to you in the way of righteousness, and you did not believe him; but tax collectors and harlots believed him; and when you saw it, you did not afterward relent and believe him."

Jesus continues His teaching on authority by describing a man and his two sons. Zibeon knows exactly what Jesus is talking about. Zibeon's father often tells Zibeon and his brother to go do some chores, in this case, to go work in the vineyard.

Zibeon's brother is a bright-eyed morning person, but he is lazy and he gets distracted easily. So, when his father gives him a task in the morning he always says, "Yes, sir." But, when it is time to go to the vineyard to work, he gets distracted along the way, daydreaming and he never gets the work done.

Zibeon is not a morning person. When his father sends him to the vineyard, he has the audacity to tell his father, "I will not." Afterwards, once Zibeon is fully awake, he feels awful. He must be thinking: *How could I disobey my father like that? Why didn't I just do it? Will my father forgive me if I go to the vineyard now?*

Jesus asks the religious leaders; "Which of the two did the will of his father?" Zibeon is pleased when the religious leaders say that the reluctant, obedient son did the will of this father. Jesus then surprises everyone by saying that the hated tax collectors and the despised harlots will enter the kingdom of God before the religious leaders. The despicable ones were all leading disobedient lives, but they repented and then did the will of their heavenly Father. The religious leaders thought that they had no need to repent.

We often forget how merciful and patient our heavenly Father is. It is never too late to repent and agree to do His will. It does not matter how long you have rebelled or how many times, God always accepts His children when they wholeheartedly repent and turn towards Him. Do you need to do this today?

Notes:

Matthew 21:33-39

Wicked Vinedressers

33 "Hear another parable: There was a certain landowner who planted a vineyard and set a hedge around it, dug a winepress in it and built a tower. And he leased it to vinedressers and went into a far country. 34 Now when vintage-time drew near, he sent his servants to the vinedressers, that they might receive its fruit. 35 And the vinedressers took his servants, beat one, killed one, and stoned another. 36 Again he sent other servants, more than the first, and they did likewise to them. 37 Then last of all he sent his son to them, saying, 'They will respect my son.' 38 But when the vinedressers saw the son, they said among themselves, 'This is the heir. Come, let us kill him and seize his inheritance.' 39 So they took him and cast him out of the vineyard and killed him."

Jesus continues focusing His teaching on the religious leaders. He tells a parable about a landowner who plants a vineyard. The religious leaders know immediately that a vineyard is a symbol for Israel in much of the Scriptures. Therefore, they correctly surmise that the landowner must be God.

The vineyard is very well prepared as it has a hedge around it for protection from animals, a winepress on the property for easy and efficient production, and a tower for protection from thieves. The landowner leases out the vineyard to others to be caretakers, just as God did in the Garden of Eden in the beginning of time, as told in the book of Genesis.

It is harvest time, so the landowner sends his servants to collect from the vinedressers. The vinedressers beat one, kill another and stone a third. The landowner cannot understand this animosity from the vinedressers. Didn't the landowner do everything that could be done to make for a good harvest?

Finally, the landowner sends his own son, for surely, "They will respect my son." The vinedressers see the son as the heir, so they kill him with the hope that they will seize his inheritance. The religious leaders immediately see that Jesus is referring to them. They have been the caretakers of the nation of Israel for years, and yet they have led God's people astray.

Isaac has been listening to this parable; He sees that it is not just for the religious leaders, but it is everyone. He knows that he has rejected God's lordship over his life time and time again. Isaac wonders, *Would I also try to kill the landlord's son? Surely not."*

We will see later that many in the crowd called for Jesus' death. Do you suppose that Isaac was there? What would you cry out if you were there?

Notes:

Matthew 22:23-33 (Part 1)

What About the Resurrection?

23 *The same day the Sadducees, who say there is no resurrection, came to Him and asked Him,* 24 *saying: "Teacher, Moses said that if a man dies, having no children, his brother shall marry his wife and raise up offspring for his brother.* 25 *Now there were with us seven brothers. The first died after he had married, and having no offspring, left his wife to his brother.* 26 *Likewise the second also, and the third, even to the seventh.* 27 *Last of all the woman died also.* 28 *Therefore, in the resurrection, whose wife of the seven will she be? For they all had her."*

29 *Jesus answered and said to them, "You are mistaken, not knowing the Scriptures nor the power of God.* 30 *For in the resurrection they neither marry nor are given in marriage, but are like angels of God in heaven.* 31 *But concerning the resurrection of the dead, have you not read what was spoken to you by God, saying,* 32 *'I am the God of Abraham, the God of Isaac, and the God of Jacob'? God is not the God of the dead, but of the living."* 33 *And when the multitudes heard this, they were astonished at His teaching.*

The Sadducees were the most liberal of the religious leaders, in contrast to the Pharisees who were the most conservative. As such, the Sadducees did not believe in the resurrection of the dead. Therefore, they posed a tricky question to Jesus about the resurrection, heaven and family units in heaven.

Jesus starts by rebuking them with, "You are mistaken." The Sadducees are mistaken in their view of the Scriptures as they only believed in the first five books of the Bible, the Torah, and not all of the Scriptures. They are greatly mistaken in their view of the power of God. Jesus teaches that the purpose of the resurrection is not for family units, but for the worship of God, as the angels do. Jesus continues by using language from Genesis where God refers to Himself by saying, "'I am the God of Abraham, the God of Isaac, and the God of Jacob," referring to the three most important forefathers of the Jewish people. Jesus says, "God is not the God of the dead, but of the living."

In the Westminster Shorter Catechism, the first question and answer are: "What is the chief end of man? Man's chief end is to glorify God, and to enjoy Him forever." God has called us to enjoy Him forever, not just in heaven but here on earth. God is the God of the living. Can you begin your time in heaven today by enjoying being in His presence?

Notes:

Matthew 22:23-33 (Part 2)

What About the Resurrection?

23 The same day the Sadducees, who say there is no resurrection, came to Him and asked Him, 24 saying: "Teacher, Moses said that if a man dies, having no children, his brother shall marry his wife and raise up offspring for his brother. 25 Now there were with us seven brothers. The first died after he had married, and having no offspring, left his wife to his brother. 26 Likewise the second also, and the third, even to the seventh. 27 Last of all the woman died also. 28 Therefore, in the resurrection, whose wife of the seven will she be? For they all had her."

29 Jesus answered and said to them, "You are mistaken, not knowing the Scriptures nor the power of God. 30 For in the resurrection they neither marry nor are given in marriage, but are like angels of God in heaven. 31 But concerning the resurrection of the dead, have you not read what was spoken to you by God, saying, 32 'I am the God of Abraham, the God of Isaac, and the God of Jacob'? God is not the God of the dead, but of the living." 33 And when the multitudes heard this, they were astonished at His teaching.

The Sadducees were very confused about heaven. *Does heaven exist? If so, who is there? Will we know each other in heaven? What will we do there?* Many of us have these same questions today.

Years after this discussion between Jesus and the Sadducees, the Christian church in the city of Corinth had lots of the same questions about the resurrection. The Apostle Paul summarized the resurrection with these points.

- Jesus did rise from the dead and was witnessed by many, by over five hundred at once
- As Christ rose from the dead, so will His believers
- We will be raised into celestial bodies that are perfected and different from our terrestrial bodies
- We will be raised to be incorruptible, unable to sin anymore
- Jesus has conquered death forever, it has no more sting

While your resurrection into heaven may be some time off, can you enjoy the fact that God gives you little glimpses of the glory of heaven even now? Can you grab hold of them and use them to be more like Jesus every day?

Notes:

Matthew 22:34-40

What Is the Great Commandment?

34 But when the Pharisees heard that He had silenced the Sadducees, they gathered together. 35 Then one of them, a lawyer, asked Him a question, testing Him, and saying, 36 "Teacher, which is the great commandment in the law?"

37 Jesus said to him, "'You shall love the LORD your God with all your heart, with all your soul, and with all your mind.' 38 This is the first and great commandment. 39 And the second is like it: 'You shall love your neighbor as yourself.' 40 On these two commandments hang all the Law and the Prophets."

Isaac is standing with his Pharisee friends and he sees that they are delighted that Jesus has put their religious rivals, the Sadducees, in their place. He silenced them. Now, they are going to silence Jesus. They appoint one of their sharpest minds to trip Jesus up with a question. The question is about the commandments. Everyone knows that there are many more commandments than the Ten Commandments in the Torah. They are hoping that Jesus will stumble over the multiplicity of choices.

Jesus responds with the Shema, which everyone knows starts with, "Hear, O Israel." It continues with, "You shall love the LORD your God with all your heart, with all your soul, and with all your mind." Isaac sees that all of the Pharisees nod approvingly. Jesus then adds in a bonus answer: the second great commandment is from Leviticus, "You shall love your neighbor as yourself."

The Pharisees are left speechless, silenced by Jesus' wisdom. Then, Isaac sees Jesus look each of the Pharisees in the eye. When Jesus looks Isaac in the eye, he hears an unmistakable voice asking: *Have you been loving God with all our heart, with all your soul, and with all your mind? Have you been loving your neighbor? Why not?*

Isaac is cut to the quick. He knows that he has not been loving God as he should. He knows that he has not been loving his neighbor as he loves himself. He knows he cannot do it on his own. In that moment he pleads with Jesus, *Will you help me?* Jesus smiles and says, "Of course I will, I am the only One who can change your heart."

If Jesus were to look you in the eye right now, concerning these two great commandments, what would you talk about?

Notes:

Matthew 23:1-36

Woe to the Scribes and Pharisees

Jesus speaks to the multitude about the religious leaders, the scribes and Pharisees, and He corrects them in a way that is also instructive to the multitude.

Jesus starts with, "Therefore whatever they tell you to observe, that observe and do, but do not do according to their works; for they say, and do not do" (Matthew 23:3). Like many of us, they talk the good talk, but when it comes down to the messy work of really loving their neighbors, they leave that to someone else.

"...All their works they do to be seen by men" (Matthew 23:5a). When they finally get around to doing some good works, they focus on doing their deeds so that others will see them and will give them the praise.

Jesus calls them "Blind guides" (Matthew 23:16a). They think that they are leading the people in God's ways, yet they have not spent time allowing God's word to take root in their hearts.

Jesus praises them in that they "...Pay tithe of mint and anise and cummin" (Matthew 23:23a), yet they neglect the weightier matters of the law. They do not focus on "Justice, mercy and faith. These you ought to have done, without leaving the others undone" (Matthew 23:23b). They do the small matters well, but the bigger, harder life issues they neglect.

Jesus describes them like a well-used coffee cup. The outside of the cup is clean and bright, but the inside is dirty and stained. They may look righteous on the outside, yet "...Inside they are full of extortion and self-indulgence" (Matthew 23:25). He tells them that if they want to be right in the kingdom of God, they must first cleanse the inside of the cup, their hearts and minds; then the outside cleansing will follow.

Jesus continues His critical statements about the religious leaders by calling them whitewashed tombs. "They appear beautiful outwardly, but inside are full of dead men's bones and all unclearness" (Matthew 23:27). Jesus says that they are filled with death inside, filled with "Hypocrisy and lawlessness" (Matthew 23:28).

Jesus ends by calling them serpents and vipers who kill the prophets and wisemen who are sent to lead the people towards God.

Jesus gives a very scathing judgment on the religious leaders of the day to the multitude. If you were in the crowd then, what would Jesus say about you?

Notes:

Matthew 24:1-2

The Destruction of the Temple

¹ Then Jesus went out and departed from the temple, and His disciples came up to show Him the buildings of the temple. ² And Jesus said to them, "Do you not see all these things? Assuredly, I say to you, not one stone shall be left here upon another, that shall not be thrown down."

Jesus has been teaching in the temple for a while and when He leaves His disciples want to give Him a tour of the temple campus. The temple was built by King Herod the Great, a Roman. He was a great architect and builder. This temple campus covered about thirty-five acres. Herod designed it to be built with massive stone blocks, many of them weighing over 100 tons. Outside the temple, the walls of the city of Jerusalem were over 150 feet tall. Everyone who saw the temple was very impressed by it. The disciples who traveled with Jesus all throughout Galilee, far to the north, expected Jesus to be very impressed by the temple. However, Jesus' response to seeing it was that "not one stone shall be left here upon another, that shall not be thrown down."

Everyone is very surprised by Jesus' statement. *Could He possibly be serious?* As it turns out, Jesus was prophesying about the Roman invasion of Jerusalem to destroy the city and the Jews in 70 AD. The Roman siege lasted six months until the city fell. The destruction of the city was so complete that the temple was totally destroyed and not one stone was left on another.

Why would Jesus say such a thing? First as a signpost to His Lordship in years to come. Many came to believe in Him forty years after His death because of this prophecy. Second, He warned the Christians several times about the upcoming destruction and to flee the city when they saw the destruction of the temple. They did and many lives were saved with this exodus. Third, He is Lord of the nations. Nations rise and fall, all under God's sovereign will.

So it is today. God is sovereign over all nations. As the Psalmist says:

Now therefore, be wise, O kings;
Be instructed, you judges of the earth.
Serve the LORD with fear,
And rejoice with trembling. (Psalm 2:10-11).

What can you do? Pray for your leaders that they may be wise and serve the LORD.

Notes:

Matthew 24:14-25

Well Done, Good and Faithful Servant

14 "For the kingdom of heaven is like a man traveling to a far country, who called his own servants and delivered his goods to them. 15 And to one he gave five talents, to another two, and to another one, to each according to his own ability; and immediately he went on a journey. 16 Then he who had received the five talents went and traded with them, and made another five talents... 18 But he who had received one went and dug in the ground, and hid his lord's money. 19 After a long time the lord of those servants came and settled accounts with them.

20 "So he who had received five talents came and brought five other talents, saying, 'Lord, you delivered to me five talents; look, I have gained five more talents besides them.' 21 His lord said to him, 'Well done, good and faithful servant; you were faithful over a few things, I will make you ruler over many things. Enter into the joy of your lord.' 22 He also who had received two talents came and said, 'Lord, you delivered to me two talents; look, I have gained two more talents besides them.' 23 His lord said to him, 'Well done, good and faithful servant; you have been faithful over a few things, I will make you ruler over many things. Enter into the joy of your lord.'

24 "Then he who had received the one talent came and said, 'Lord, I knew you to be a hard man, reaping where you have not sown, and gathering where you have not scattered seed. 25 And I was afraid, and went and hid your talent in the ground. Look, there you have what is yours.'"

Jesus tells His disciples another parable about the kingdom of heaven. In this parable a lord was going to travel to a far country and he gave three of his servants incredible gifts to use, as each talent was worth about fifteen years of salary. Talents are meant to be used: to build a life, and to do good for others.

The first and second servants were given five and two talents, incredible gifts. They used their talents in a great way. They worked, they worried, and they traded so that they doubled their worth. The third servant was given one talent, still a vast sum. Unfortunately, he did not use his talent and the lord was very displeased with him.

So it is with us today. God has given us incredible talents. We can use our talents as artists, plumbers, researchers, teachers, and so much more. God expects us to use the talents that He has given us. At the end of time, when you stand before God, will He say, "Well done, good and faithful servant"? If you are not on that path, what will it take to get there?

Notes:

Matthew 25:31-40

Sheep and Goats

31 "When the Son of Man comes in His glory, and all the holy angels with Him, then He will sit on the throne of His glory. 32 All the nations will be gathered before Him, and He will separate them one from another, as a shepherd divides his sheep from the goats. 33 And He will set the sheep on His right hand, but the goats on the left. 34 Then the King will say to those on His right hand, 'Come, you blessed of My Father, inherit the kingdom prepared for you from the foundation of the world: 35 for I was hungry and you gave Me food; I was thirsty and you gave Me drink; I was a stranger and you took Me in; 36 I was naked and you clothed Me; I was sick and you visited Me; I was in prison and you came to Me.'

37 "Then the righteous will answer Him, saying, 'Lord, when did we see You hungry and feed You, or thirsty and give You drink? 38 When did we see You a stranger and take You in, or naked and clothe You? 39 Or when did we see You sick, or in prison, and come to You?' 40 And the King will answer and say to them, 'Assuredly, I say to you, inasmuch as you did it to one of the least of these My brethren, you did it to Me.'"

Jesus tells His disciples about the end of time when He will come into His glory. He will sit on the throne of His glory and everyone will come before Him. He describes His believers as sheep and the non-believers as goats. Instead of focusing on the state of the heart, which only He can see, He focuses on the deeds that flow out of the heart. Jesus has made it clear previously that He is only concerned with the state of the heart. Is it turned towards Him and in love with Him or is it turned towards self and in love with self?

In this case, He uses actions towards others as a way to see the state of the heart. The actions in question are all actions done for the lowly that cannot be repaid. They are good works done for the hungry, the thirsty, the strangers, those naked, the sick, and those in prison. All who had no ability to pay back the good deed. These are just examples of what it means to love your neighbor as yourself.

To inherit the kingdom prepared for you, there are two simple steps. The first is to surrender your heart to Jesus as your Lord and Savior. The second is to then go live a life filled with gratitude. At the end of your time, will the Lord say to you, "Come, you blessed of My Father"?

Notes:

164

Matthew 26:6-13

A Great Gift to Be Remembered

6 And when Jesus was in Bethany at the house of Simon the leper, 7 a woman came to Him having an alabaster flask of very costly fragrant oil, and she poured it on His head as He sat at the table. 8 But when His disciples saw it, they were indignant, saying, "Why this waste? 9 For this fragrant oil might have been sold for much and given to the poor."

10 But when Jesus was aware of it, He said to them, "Why do you trouble the woman? For she has done a good work for Me. 11 For you have the poor with you always, but Me you do not have always. 12 For in pouring this fragrant oil on My body, she did it for My burial. 13 Assuredly, I say to you, wherever this gospel is preached in the whole world, what this woman has done will also be told as a memorial to her."

Jesus is staying in Bethany, which is just a few miles south of Jerusalem. Simon, one of the many former-lepers healed by Jesus, is hosting Jesus and His disciples for a dinner party. Simon is so very grateful to Jesus for His merciful healing. Simon knows that he does not deserve God's mercy. He knows many friends who still have great troubles and sickness. Therefore, Simon goes about each day being grateful for what God has done and his gratitude is visible to those around him.

That may be one of the reasons that Simon allows this woman to be at the dinner party. She too wants to show her gratitude to Jesus. In this case, she takes a very costly jar of fragrant oil and pours it on Jesus' head as a way of symbolizing the anointing for His burial. Of course, the disciples do not understand this at all, they only see the waste. It is almost a year's worth of salary. It could have greatly helped the poor.

Simon, who is listening to Jesus' discussion with His disciples, learns several things. The first is to always be grateful. Always be ready to show your gratitude for what God has done for you. The second is that Jesus did not come to abolish poverty. There will always be poor people. If you want to abolish poverty, start by befriending just one poor family. The third is to acknowledge that Jesus died for you. This woman is anointing Jesus as the Messiah, the One who came to die unjustly at the hands of sinners to pay the penalty for her sins. She is acknowledging His rule over her life.

Do you have something or some talent that you need to give wholeheartedly to Jesus? Is there some way that you can show your gratitude? This woman did and she will be remembered throughout the whole world for all time.

Notes:

Matthew 26:14-16

Betrayer!

14 Then one of the twelve, called Judas Iscariot, went to the chief priests 15 and said, "What are you willing to give me if I deliver Him to you?" And they counted out to him thirty pieces of silver. 16 So from that time he sought opportunity to betray Him.

Judas Iscariot! He is the most infamous betrayer in the history of the world. Why did he do it? We don't really know, but we do know a great deal about Judas.

We know in calling of the twelve disciples: "He [Jesus] went out to the mountain to pray, and continued all night in prayer to God" (Luke 6:12). Jesus must have prayed over each of the disciples individually, by name. He probably prayed for wisdom, strength, their individual ministries, and protection from the evil one. His prayer over Judas must have been especially agonizing.

Judas spent three years traveling throughout Galilee and then to Jerusalem with Jesus and the other eleven disciples. He must have heard most of Jesus' teachings, sermons, and parable stories. Many of them must have touched Judas' heart deeply.

However, Judas has a money problem. John tells us that Judas does not really care for the poor, "...because he was a thief, and had the money box, and he used to take what was put in it" (John 12:6b). Apparently, Judas would skim a little off of the top of any offerings the disciples received. Judas may have done this for years, perhaps a little more each time. Judas' desire for money got so strong that he sought out the chief priests and said, "What are you willing to give me if I deliver Him to you?" Judas got thirty pieces of silver, which is the going price for a slave in the marketplace. Here we see how all-consuming Judas' love for money was, that he would betray his best friend in the world for thirty pieces of silver.

We wonder if there is anyone else like Judas. As we think about this, we realize that we are betrayers just like Judas. For us it may not be money, it may be our pride, our place in society, our job, or our view of our self-worth. We are willing to sacrifice these things at the altar of our idol gods instead of giving our hearts fully over to Jesus' Lordship. Look in the mirror of your heart today and acknowledge your areas of betrayal.

Can you repent and give these areas over to Jesus before it is too late?

Notes:

Matthew 26:31-35

I Will Not Deny You

31 Then Jesus said to them, "All of you will be made to stumble because of Me this night, for it is written:

'I will strike the Shepherd,
And the sheep of the flock will be scattered.'

32 But after I have been raised, I will go before you to Galilee." 33 Peter answered and said to Him, "Even if all are made to stumble because of You, I will never be made to stumble." 34 Jesus said to him, "Assuredly, I say to you that this night, before the rooster crows, you will deny Me three times. 35 Peter said to Him, "Even if I have to die with You, I will not deny You!"

Jesus has just finished eating the last Passover meal with His disciples. He is leading them to the Mount of Olives and He says that all of them will stumble. He says that it has been prophesied by Zechariah that the Shepherd will be struck and the sheep will scatter. However, after He has been raised, He will meet them back in their hometown region of Galilee.

Peter, always the impulsive one, says that he will never stumble, even if all of the other disciples stumble. Jesus tells Peter that he will deny Him not once, but three times this very night. From Luke's Gospel we read: "Indeed, Satan has asked for you, that he may sift you as wheat. But I have prayed for you, that your faith should not fail; and when you have returned to Me, strengthen your brethren" (Luke 22:31-32).

Satan has asked for permission to sift Peter like wheat. Jesus tells Peter to hold onto hope. Yes, Peter will deny his Lord Jesus, not once, but three times. Yes, Satan will attack Peter and he will feel like all is lost. But Jesus tells him that his faith will not fail because Peter has a greater purpose to come, to strengthen the new believers.

So it is with us. There will be difficult times ahead. Perhaps a great Christian friend will betray you or abandon you. Perhaps you will feel like your flock has scattered and you are alone. Perhaps there will be a time or two where you will stumble. Do not lose hope, ever. Know this for sure:

What then shall we say to these things? If God is for us, who can be against us? He who did not spare His own Son, but delivered Him up for us all, how shall He not with Him also freely give us all things? Who shall bring a charge against God's elect? It is God who justifies. Who is he who condemns? It is Christ who died, and furthermore is also risen, who is even at the right hand of God, who also makes intercession for us.
(Romans 8:31-34).

Can you hold on to the incredible fact that Jesus is interceding for you before the Father?

Notes:

Matthew 26:36-39

As You Will

36 Then Jesus came with them to a place called Gethsemane, and said to the disciples, "Sit here while I go and pray over there." 37 And He took with Him Peter and the two sons of Zebedee, and He began to be sorrowful and deeply distressed. 38 Then He said to them, "My soul is exceedingly sorrowful, even to death. Stay here and watch with Me."

39 He went a little farther and fell on His face, and prayed, saying, "O My Father, if it is possible, let this cup pass from Me; nevertheless, not as I will, but as You will."

Peter saw that Jesus was distressed when He asked him, James, and John to join Him in Gethsemane. Jesus told them to stay in one place while He went off by Himself to pray. Even from a distance, Peter could tell that Jesus was deeply distressed.

If Peter could have stayed awake, he would have heard Jesus pleading with His Father so that the cup of the Father's wrath could pass from Him. The cup represented all of the sins of God's people, all of the sins that you and I have committed and will commit. Jesus' human nature was pleading with the Father, if it was possible for the cup to pass. Even from His exceedingly sorrowful state, Jesus knew that it was not His will that mattered, but only the will of His Father.

If Peter could have stayed awake, he would have learned a great deal about prayer. First, Jesus went off by Himself. In this time of heart-wrenching prayer, He needed to be alone with the Father. While it is great to pray with others, sometimes we need to be alone with the Father so that we can speak directly from the heart and allow ourselves to be totally exposed to the Father. Second, Jesus clearly expressed what His will was. His human nature wanted to know if it was possible for the cup of wrath to pass Him by. He probably wrestled with this thought and all of those emotions for quite a while in prayer. He ended His time with "Not as I will, but as You will." This is the nature of true prayer. We bring our thoughts and hopes and desires to the Father and then we stop and listen to understand His will. That is what true prayer is, aligning our wills with the Father's will.

The next time you are in deep and sorrowful prayer, can you pray like Jesus and seek to align with the Father's will?

Notes:

Matthew 26:47-53

Commander of the Angel Armies

47 And while He was still speaking, behold, Judas, one of the twelve, with a great multitude with swords and clubs, came from the chief priests and elders of the people. 48 Now His betrayer had given them a sign, saying, "Whomever I kiss, He is the One; seize Him." 49 Immediately he went up to Jesus and said, "Greetings, Rabbi!" and kissed Him. 50 But Jesus said to him, "Friend, why have you come?" Then they came and laid hands on Jesus and took Him. 51 And suddenly, one of those who were with Jesus stretched out his hand and drew his sword, struck the servant of the high priest, and cut off his ear. 52 But Jesus said to him, "Put your sword in its place, for all who take the sword will perish by the sword. 53 Or do you think that I cannot now pray to My Father, and He will provide Me with more than twelve legions of angels?"

Judas is betraying Jesus by leading a great multitude from the chief priests and the elders. They are all prepared for war, armed with swords and homemade clubs. Isaac is on the edge, but he is swept along with the crowd. He is surprised by a few things. Why are they looking for Jesus at night? Why do they look like they are preparing for war?

Isaac watches as Judas greets Jesus with a brotherly kiss. Jesus then asks him, "Friend, why have you come?" Is Jesus just asking Judas, or is He asking every individual, including Isaac, in the crowd? Isaac asks himself, *Why have I come?*

All of a sudden, chaos breaks out. Several of them are grabbing Jesus and handling Him roughly. One of the disciples stretches out his hand and strikes one of the servants of the high priest. Isaac wonders, *Are we really at war with Jesus?*

Jesus takes control of the situation with His words. He reminds everyone that He can call down twelve legions of angels. With that one phrase, Jesus reminds Isaac of the time Elisha was near Dothan, surrounded by the enemies from Syria and his servant was afraid of the war ahead. Elisha prayed that his servant's eyes would be opened and "Then the LORD opened the eyes of the young man, and he saw. And behold, the mountain was full of horses and chariots of fire all around Elisha" (2 Kings 6:17b).

Isaac understands immediately that this is a spiritual war. While Jesus is the Commander of the angel armies, now is not the time for their attack. Jesus must submit to the chief priests, for now. You too are in the middle of a spiritual war. You cannot defeat the enemy on your own. Will you rely on the Commander of the angel armies?

Notes:

Matthew 26:59-66 (Part 1)

Are You the Christ?

⁵⁹ Now the chief priests, the elders, and all the council sought false testimony against Jesus to put Him to death, ⁶⁰ but found none. Even though many false witnesses came forward, they found none. But at last two false witnesses came forward ⁶¹ and said, "This fellow said, 'I am able to destroy the temple of God and to build it in three days.'"

⁶² And the high priest arose and said to Him, "Do You answer nothing? What is it these men testify against You?" ⁶³ But Jesus kept silent. And the high priest answered and said to Him, "I put You under oath by the living God: Tell us if You are the Christ, the Son of God!"

⁶⁴ Jesus said to him, "It is as you said. Nevertheless, I say to you, hereafter you will see the Son of Man sitting at the right hand of the Power, and coming on the clouds of heaven."

⁶⁵ Then the high priest tore his clothes, saying, "He has spoken blasphemy! What further need do we have of witnesses? Look, now you have heard His blasphemy! ⁶⁶ What do you think?"

They answered and said, "He is deserving of death."

Isaac follows at a distance as the multitude takes Jesus to the home of the high priest, Caiaphas. Isaac is very confused. First, all of Jesus' disciples have scattered in fear. Now there is an assembly of the scribes and elders but it is at night, and at Caiaphas' house. Isaac knows from his Pharisee school that this is most improper. They are supposed to meet in the Temple, at a pre-arranged meeting time, and during the daytime. Then there were many uncorroborated witnesses, who all knew the penalty for bearing false witness, the expected penalty of the accused, in this case death!

The high priest is getting upset that his kangaroo court is not getting the result that he wants, so he attacks Jesus: "Do You answer nothing?" Jesus remains silent as Isaiah prophesied long ago:

He was oppressed and He was afflicted,
Yet He opened not His mouth;
He was led as a lamb to the slaughter,
And as a sheep before its shearers is silent,
So He opened not His mouth.
(Isaiah 53:7)

When your time comes, will you be able to bear a true witness to who Jesus is?

Notes:

Matthew 26:59-66 (Part 2)

Are You the Christ?

59 Now the chief priests, the elders, and all the council sought false testimony against Jesus to put Him to death, 60 but found none. Even though many false witnesses came forward, they found none. But at last two false witnesses came forward 61 and said, "This fellow said, 'I am able to destroy the temple of God and to build it in three days.'"

62 And the high priest arose and said to Him, "Do You answer nothing? What is it these men testify against You?" 63 But Jesus kept silent. And the high priest answered and said to Him, "I put You under oath by the living God: Tell us if You are the Christ, the Son of God!"

64 Jesus said to him, "It is as you said. Nevertheless, I say to you, hereafter you will see the Son of Man sitting at the right hand of the Power, and coming on the clouds of heaven."

65 Then the high priest tore his clothes, saying, "He has spoken blasphemy! What further need do we have of witnesses? Look, now you have heard His blasphemy! 66 What do you think?"

They answered and said, "He is deserving of death."

Being frustrated, Caiaphas commands Jesus directly, "Tell us if You are the Christ, the Son of God!" Isaac hears Jesus calmly proclaim, "It is as you said." Isaac thinks, *Finally, now all of the important religious leaders will acknowledge Jesus as the long-awaited Messiah.* However, the high priest tears his clothes in protest. Isaac is very confused. Doesn't the high priest realize what Nicodemus realized when he said to Jesus, "No one can do these signs that You do unless God is with him?" Isaac leaves totally dejected. *How can they be so blind? They saw the miracles that Jesus did. They heard Him acknowledge that He is the Messiah. What more do they want?*

In their blind arrogance, they would rather condemn an innocent man to death than believe their own eyes and ears and hearts.

How about you? Have you seen and heard enough to acknowledge Jesus as your Lord and Master?

Notes:

Matthew 26:69-74

How Could I Deny Him?

69 Now Peter sat outside in the courtyard. And a servant girl came to him, saying, "You also were with Jesus of Galilee."

70 But he denied it before them all, saying, "I do not know what you are saying."

71 And when he had gone out to the gateway, another girl saw him and said to those who were there, "This fellow also was with Jesus of Nazareth."

72 But again he denied with an oath, "I do not know the Man!"

73 And a little later those who stood by came up and said to Peter, "Surely you also are one of them, for your speech betrays you."

74 Then he began to curse and swear, saying, "I do not know the Man!"

Peter is once again following Jesus, but this time at a distance and in fear. He is in the outer courtyard of Caiaphas' house. A young, servant girl comes up to Peter and declares that she recognizes him as one of Jesus' followers. Even though she has no authority over Peter, he denies it and lies to this young, servant girl. He is confronted by a second girl, and finally, a little later, by someone who recognizes his Galilean accent. Peter declares, "I do not know the Man!"

Luke tells us that after the rooster crowed, "The Lord turned and looked at Peter" (Luke 22:61). The gospel writers then give us one of the greatest understatements: "He [Peter] went out and wept bitterly."

Peter must have remembered his many good times with Jesus. *Being so overjoyed when Jesus called him to join Him to be a fisher of men. How Jesus taught him every day to be the salt of the earth and the light of the world. How Jesus never ridiculed him when he made a mistake or sinned. How Jesus showed him pure mercy when He healed his wife's mother, which did so much to strength his faith and his relationship with his wife. Jesus taught him and Andrew, his brother, about His yoke and how it makes doing God's work easier, like having a good rowing partner. He even allowed him to see His transfigured glory and then hear God the Father speak. How could he be so foolish as to deny Him?*

Can you take some time today to remember all that God has done for you?

Notes:

Matthew 27:15-23

Let Him Be Crucified

¹⁵ Now at the feast the governor was accustomed to releasing to the multitude one prisoner whom they wished. ¹⁶ And at that time they had a notorious prisoner called Barabbas. ¹⁷ Therefore, when they had gathered together, Pilate said to them, "Whom do you want me to release to you? Barabbas, or Jesus who is called Christ?" ¹⁸ For he knew that they had handed Him over because of envy. ¹⁹ While he was sitting on the judgment seat, his wife sent to him, saying, "Have nothing to do with that just Man, for I have suffered many things today in a dream because of Him."²⁰ But the chief priests and elders persuaded the multitudes that they should ask for Barabbas and destroy Jesus. ²¹ The governor answered and said to them, "Which of the two do you want me to release to you?" They said, "Barabbas!" ²² Pilate said to them, "What then shall I do with Jesus who is called Christ?" They all said to him, "Let Him be crucified!" ²³ Then the governor said, "Why, what evil has He done?" But they cried out all the more, saying, "Let Him be crucified!"

Peter has somewhat recovered from his great denial of his Lord and Messiah, Jesus; so, he follows Jesus' trial before Pilate. It is the time of the great Passover feast; therefore, Pilate, the governor, releases one prisoner to placate the Jews. Peter is sure that Jesus will be released and this whole recent nightmare will be over. Pilate makes it easy for the Jews; it is a choice between only two men. Barabbas is a despicable person, a convicted murderer. Jesus has done no wrong, He has only helped and healed people.

However, the religious establishment has enticed the crowd to ask for Barabbas. Pilate is somewhat surprised by this and so he asks, "What then shall I do with Jesus who is called Christ?" Peter cannot believe that all of those around him are screaming, "Let Him be crucified!" Pilate asks them, "Why, what evil has He done?" Peter says to himself, *Finally, Pilate will knock some sense into the people.* However, to avoid a riot, Pilate takes the easy way out and sends an innocent man to be crucified.

For the second time in two days Peter weeps bitterly. This time it is because Peter cannot stop the violence of the crowd. He does not shout at Pilate to do the right thing. He does not volunteer to take Jesus' place. Peter finally grasps what it means for Jesus to be God's Messiah. He came in the person of a human baby, even though He was One with God. He lived a sinless life helping, healing, and teaching. He chooses to die in Peter's place. If you were in the crowd that day, how would you have reacted?

Notes:

Matthew 27:36-43

Save Yourself

36 Sitting down, they kept watch over Him there. 37 And they put up over His head the accusation written against Him:

THIS IS JESUS THE KING OF THE JEWS.

38 Then two robbers were crucified with Him, one on the right and another on the left.

39 And those who passed by blasphemed Him, wagging their heads 40 and saying, "You who destroy the temple and build it in three days, save Yourself! If You are the Son of God, come down from the cross."

41 Likewise the chief priests also, mocking with the scribes and elders, said, 42 "He saved others; Himself He cannot save. If He is the King of Israel, let Him now come down from the cross, and we will believe Him. 43 He trusted in God; let Him deliver Him now if He will have Him; for He said, 'I am the Son of God.'"

Jesus has been whipped, mocked, and crowned with a crown of thorns. He is placed on a cross in Golgotha. Quite a large group of people has come to witness this horrible deed. Many of the people who pass by continue to mock and blaspheme Him. Their most common scorn is, "Save Yourself."

Luke is in the crowd. He cannot believe his ears. He was there when Jesus healed the leper. The leper knew that he could not save himself, he needed Jesus to save him.

It is the same with the Roman centurion. He knew that he could not save his servant who was at home, paralyzed and tormented. He also knew that his servant could not save himself. The centurion needed Jesus to speak a word of salvation.

The four friends of Rueben, the healed paralytic friend, knew that he could not save himself. Therefore, they lowered him through a hole in the roof. Jesus not only saved him physically, but He saved him spiritually when He forgave his sins.

Peter saw Jesus walking on the water during the storm; he joined Jesus on the water, but quickly sank. Peter cried out, "Lord, save me!"

They all followed Jesus one way or another and they all learned one thing: they could not save themselves; only Jesus can save them. Yet, here is Jesus on the cross uniquely able to save Himself, and He freely gives up His life to save us. He is indeed the King. Who will you trust each and every day to save you; yourself or the King?

Notes:

Matthew 27:45-50

Forsaken

45 Now from the sixth hour until the ninth hour there was darkness over all the land. 46 And about the ninth hour Jesus cried out with a loud voice, saying, "Eli, Eli, lama sabachthani?" that is, "My God, My God, why have You forsaken Me?"

47 Some of those who stood there, when they heard that, said, "This Man is calling for Elijah!" 48 Immediately one of them ran and took a sponge, filled it with sour wine and put it on a reed, and offered it to Him to drink.

49 The rest said, "Let Him alone; let us see if Elijah will come to save Him."

50 And Jesus cried out again with a loud voice, and yielded up His spirit.

Jesus is Immanuel, God with us. He is the long-awaited Messiah. He is described by John: "In the beginning was the Word, and the Word was with God, and the Word was God" (John 1:1). He is also fully human, born as a baby to the virgin Mary. While the details of Immanuel are a bit of a mystery, we do know many things about Jesus, Immanuel.

Jesus lived among us. He breathed our air and drank our water. He got tired and slept in boats. He bled real blood on the cross. He also traveled throughout Israel teaching, healing, and performing many great signs that pointed to His God nature. He lived a sinless, perfect life, always obedient to the will of the Father, even to the point of drinking fully the cup of the wrath of the Father. What is this wrath? It is God's punishment for all of the sins of God's people: all of the sins that we have committed, are committing, and will commit. It is only through Jesus paying the penalty for our sins and us taking on His righteousness that we can enter the kingdom of God.

But why did Jesus quote Psalm 22:1 when He said, "My God, My God, why have You forsaken Me?" This is because, at this moment in time, the human part of Immanuel was becoming the ultimate sin-offering-goat being sacrificed for the sins of God's People (Leviticus 16:15) and He was also becoming the ultimate scapegoat taking all of the transgressions of God's people and then being driven out into the wilderness, forsaken forever (Leviticus 16:21). When the human part of Immanuel took all of the sins of God's people, He died and yielded up His spirit. Immanuel is "The Lamb of God who takes away the sin of the world."

If you have not given Him your sins, will you do it now?

Notes:

Matthew 27:50-54

Torn in Two

50 And Jesus cried out again with a loud voice, and yielded up His spirit.

51 Then, behold, the veil of the temple was torn in two from top to bottom; and the earth quaked, and the rocks were split, 52 and the graves were opened; and many bodies of the saints who had fallen asleep were raised; 53 and coming out of the graves after His resurrection, they went into the holy city and appeared to many.

54 So when the centurion and those with him, who were guarding Jesus, saw the earthquake and the things that had happened, they feared greatly, saying, "Truly this was the Son of God!"

Isaac is in the temple praying on that dark Friday. He had seen so much in the last three years. He had hoped that the traveling rabbi, Jesus, was indeed the long-awaited Messiah, come to save God's people. However, it seems not to be true. Jesus was crucified like a common criminal. How can He be the Messiah?

As Isaac is praying, he hears a great tearing sound. He cannot understand what it is. Many of the temple priests are running around in panic and confusion. They seem to be yelling, "It is torn in two!" Isaac takes this as an opportunity to investigate and so he sneaks into the Holy Place. There are some priests wailing and prostrating on their faces. Isaac peeks around them towards the Most Holy Place, the Holy of Holies. He cannot believe his eyes; the veil of the temple, which is a rich and heavy curtain that is always closed, as it protects the Most Holy Place, is torn in two from top to bottom. Isaac thinks: *The Temple veil is never, never, I mean never, open and now it is torn in two and I can see into the Most Holy Place. I can see the ark of the covenant! I can see it and I am not stuck down dead! It looks like I could have access to the Most Holy Place, the ark of the covenant, and the mercy seat, the place of the presence of God.*

Isaac rejoices greatly! *Jesus really is the Messiah! He is the Lamb of God who takes away the sin of the world; He takes away my sin.* Isaac leaves the temple and sees graves split open. He sees the Roman centurion worshiping Jesus as the Messiah. Isaac sees this as the clearest sign for all of the Jews that Jesus is the Son of God. There is no need to try to repair the temple veil; the only way forward is to accept Jesus as the Messiah.

Can you see that the veil in your life has also been torn in two? Can you see that you can now just walk through into the light of the Lamb of God?

Notes:

Matthew 27:62-66, 28:11-13

While We Slept

62 On the next day, which followed the Day of Preparation, the chief priests and Pharisees gathered together to Pilate, 63 saying, "Sir, we remember, while He was still alive, how that deceiver said, 'After three days I will rise.' 64 Therefore command that the tomb be made secure until the third day, lest His disciples come by night and steal Him away, and say to the people, 'He has risen from the dead.' So the last deception will be worse than the first."

65 Pilate said to them, "You have a guard; go your way, make it as secure as you know how." 66 So they went and made the tomb secure, sealing the stone and setting the guard.

11 Now while they were going, behold, some of the guard came into the city and reported to the chief priests all the things that had happened. 12 When they had assembled with the elders and consulted together, they gave a large sum of money to the soldiers, 13 saying, "Tell them, 'His disciples came at night and stole Him away while we slept.'"

Chaos is reigning. Jesus was buried, but some people are reporting that His body is missing.

The chief priests believe that it is time for damage control. They meet with Pilate and review some of Jesus' teachings. They tell Pilate that Jesus said, "After three days I will rise." Jesus is buried in a well-marked tomb owned by Joseph of Arimathea. They reason with Pilate that some of Jesus' crazy followers might try to steal Jesus' body from the tomb and then claim that He rose from the dead. Therefore, Pilate assigns an elite set of Roman guards to secure the tomb.

The next day people are reporting that the stone in front of the tomb is rolled back, the tomb is empty, and several people have seen a resurrected Jesus. Neither the Romans nor the religious elders can have this. Therefore, they bribe the Roman soldiers to say that the body was stolen as they slept. At first the soldiers absolutely refuse the bribe. Everyone knows that Roman soldiers do not sleep while on guard duty, ever! It would be an absolute disgrace for them to tell their fellow soldiers that they fell asleep while on guard duty. Their commanding officers order them to take the bribe and to tell the false story. In utter shame they report the story that they were asleep during the theft.

Was Jesus' body stolen, did He just walk out, or did He rise from the dead? Those seem to be the only options. Can you share your view with someone else today?

Notes:

Matthew 28:1-10

He Is Risen

¹ Now after the Sabbath, as the first day of the week began to dawn, Mary Magdalene and the other Mary came to see the tomb. ² And behold, there was a great earthquake; for an angel of the Lord descended from heaven, and came and rolled back the stone from the door, and sat on it. ³ His countenance was like lightning, and his clothing as white as snow. ⁴ And the guards shook for fear of him, and became like dead men.

⁵ But the angel answered and said to the women, "Do not be afraid, for I know that you seek Jesus who was crucified. ⁶ He is not here; for He is risen, as He said. Come, see the place where the Lord lay. ⁷ And go quickly and tell His disciples that He is risen from the dead, and indeed He is going before you into Galilee; there you will see Him. Behold, I have told you."

⁸ So they went out quickly from the tomb with fear and great joy, and ran to bring His disciples word.

⁹ And as they went to tell His disciples, behold, Jesus met them, saying, "Rejoice!" So they came and held Him by the feet and worshiped Him. ¹⁰ Then Jesus said to them,

"Do not be afraid. Go and tell My brethren to go to Galilee, and there they will see Me."

Mary Magdalene and the other Mary have heard all of the rumors; the veil in the temple is torn, graves are open, and Roman guards fell asleep. Even with all of the rumors, they go to the tomb to anoint Jesus' burial, as that is the Jewish custom.

When the women arrive at the tomb there is an angel there, whose countenance is like lighting. He tells them, "Do not be afraid." Jesus is not here; he is risen from the dead. This fantastic news is believed by the women. They leave with great joy in their hearts, running to tell the disciples.

As they go to tell the disciples, Jesus Himself appears to them in His resurrected body. He tells them to rejoice and all of the pain and grief of the last few days is washed away. Jesus tells them not to be afraid. They are to go. Don't stay here, there is nothing else; but go where I am sending you. Then, they are to tell. In this case, tell the disciples that He is risen.

So it is with us. He is risen. Our task is simple: go and tell. You can start with the fact that the tomb was empty. What story takes the most faith to believe? Was the body stolen, did Jesus walk out, or did He rise from the dead. Can you allow others to see the joy in your heart because you know that He is risen?

Notes:

Matthew 28:16-20

I Am with You Always

16 Then the eleven disciples went away into Galilee, to the mountain which Jesus had appointed for them. 17 When they saw Him, they worshiped Him; but some doubted.

18 And Jesus came and spoke to them, saying, "All authority has been given to Me in heaven and on earth. 19 Go therefore and make disciples of all the nations, baptizing them in the name of the Father and of the Son and of the Holy Spirit, 20 teaching them to observe all things that I have commanded you; and lo, I am with you always, even to the end of the age." Amen.

The disciples leave Jerusalem and travel almost eighty miles back to Galilee. Many of them are still struggling with Jesus and His resurrection. *Is He really the Messiah? Why didn't He overthrow the Romans? What does He have for me to do now? Do I go back to my previous job or does He have something new for me?*

After they arrive in Galilee, Jesus speaks with them and reassures them. He answers their questions. He tells them that He reigns again in heaven. He has all authority in heaven and on earth. He is indeed the King of kings and Lord of lords. They are now to go. There are to go and make more followers, more students. They are to share all that

He has taught them and will continue to teach them. They are not to be afraid for Jesus says, "Lo, I am with you always, even to the end of the age."

We have walked with some of the early followers of Jesus. We have seen many great miracles. We have heard many great teachings. Perhaps most important, we have seen many changed lives.

How about you? How has Jesus changed your life? Where will you go and who will you tell?

Notes:

Epilogue

The Beatitudes from the Sermon on the Mount

The Beatitudes are one of Jesus' best descriptions of what it means to live a life dedicated to God and filled with joy.

Now that we have walked with Jesus for a while, we will go back and look at a beginning section of his most famous sermon.

Matthew 5:1-3

Poor in Spirit

1 And seeing the multitudes, He went up on a mountain, and when He was seated His disciples came to Him. 2 Then He opened His mouth and taught them, saying:

3 "Blessed are the poor in spirit,
For theirs is the kingdom of heaven."

Everyone in town is really excited because the traveling rabbi, Jesus, has come to the area. He has gone a bit outside of town, up to the hillside. Everyone calls it a mountain because it is the highest point around, but it is really a large hill in front of a large grassy meadow. It is a perfect place to teach from because the teacher's voice carries very well off of the mountain down into the meadow.

Jesus begins each of His messages with "Blessed." This is a complex and rich word that translates into happy, fortunate, highly favored, admired, or simply congratulations. It is wonderful to be blessed. But blessed to be poor? Jesus then adds that He means the poor in spirit. Immediately, each person searches his own soul asking himself, *Am I poor in spirit? Do I know that I need God? Do I know that I am worthless without God in my life? Do I really love Him with all of my heart and soul? Am I lacking in my spiritual life?*

What Jesus is telling them is that if they recognize their spiritual poverty, then they are ready for the kingdom of heaven. They all remembered David's prayer before gathering the materials for the first temple in Jerusalem, David prayed,

Blessed are You, Lord God of Israel, our
*   Father, forever and ever.*
Yours, O Lord, is the greatness,
The power and the glory,
The victory and the majesty;
For all that is in heaven and in earth is Yours;
Yours is the kingdom, O Lord,
And You are exalted as head over all.
(I Chronicles 29:11)

David exults in the Lord's greatness, glory, and majesty. Jesus is telling everyone that if they recognize their spiritual poverty, their need for God, then He will share His kingdom with them. Later in Jesus' ministry He will tell them that being a part of the kingdom of heaven means that God adopts them as His children into His family.

Have you looked at your spiritual bank account recently? Do you think it is full of your so-called good deeds? Or do you see it as empty? Only when you fully understand your spiritual poverty and God's greatness can you come into His kingdom. How do you see your spiritual bank account today?

Notes:

Matthew 5:4

Mourning and Comfort

⁴ Blessed are those who mourn,
For they shall be comforted.

Daniel does not want to go to hear the new traveling rabbi who has come to town. He has just lost his grandmother and he does not want to go anywhere. Nana was his favorite and he thought that he was hers as well. He really enjoyed hearing her stories about the old days. He especially liked the stories that she told him about Abraham, Moses, and Joseph. His favorite stories were about how Joseph helped everyone: the Egyptian people as well as his own nasty brothers. Daniel often wonders how he would deal with his brothers if they played such a horrible trick on him. What would he do if they sold him into slavery and then told their father that he was killed by a wild animal? What a terrible thing to do!

As Daniel thinks about this, he begins to see what the rabbi might be talking about. Mourning is so much more than being sorry that you have lost someone. It also means being sorry for who you are. Daniel begins to think about how he has been treating his brothers recently. He begins to see that he is often irritated by them and loses his temper. Sure, he loves them, but he often wishes that they would just leave him alone, and just be gone. He then realizes that he is not very different from Joseph's brothers. He begins to weep, not just for the loss of his grandmother, but for the glimpse of his own heart that she helped him see. For the first time in his life, he is truly sorry for the things he does to his brothers and how he treats them. Just then, the rabbi completes the phrase with, "For they shall be comforted." Daniel now understands that his grandmother could never completely comfort him, deep down. Only God can comfort him there, but only when he is ready to mourn his own spiritual condition.

Has God taken you to a place where you are in mourning over some of the things that you have done, or more important, who you have become? If so, will you confess this to Him to receive His comfort?

Notes:

Matthew 5:5

Blessed Are the Meek

⁵ Blessed are the meek,
For they shall inherit the earth.

Judah is not too excited about going with his parents to hear this new travelling rabbi, Jesus. He was hoping to play with his friends today, recreating one of the great battles of Israel against the Midianites. Well at least this rabbi is in the hill country, which is a great place for imagining battles.

Judah's interest is captured by the phrase, "Blessed are the meek." He is immediately reminded of some of the great heroes of Israel, particularly Gideon.

Gideon is his all-time favorite hero because Gideon shows great meekness. Judah's father has taught him that meekness is not weakness, in fact it is quite the opposite. It means to have power, but power that is harnessed and under control. Someone who is meek knows that real power comes from God alone. God uses the meek in surprising ways, largely because they are willing to rely on the power that God gives them when they are His vessel.

Judah remembers the story of Gideon when the angel first appeared to him; Gideon could not believe the proclamation, "The LORD is with you" (Judges 6:12). Gideon's response was, "How can I save Israel? I am the least in my father's house and we are from the weakest clan." Gideon knew that he had no great saving power in himself, so he asked God for a sign. The first sign was fire from the angel's staff that consumed the meat and grain offering (Judges 6:21).

Gideon knew that God was going to use him to do a mighty work. So, when Gideon was told to tear down the altar of Baal, he took some men to help him and they did it. They did it at night because they feared the men of the city, but also because Gideon was not arrogant and boastful with his power. He knew how to be meek, how to be confident in his power and authority and God's hand in it.

In Gideon's great battle against the Midianites, God told Gideon that he had too many men. God said that if there were too many men, Israel would claim the glory for itself (Judges 7:2). God wanted Gideon to really understand meekness, power and authority that is tempered by a gracious, confident spirit that God can bring. Gideon started out with 32,000 men and they were reduced to 10,000 men, but that was still too many. God further reduced the number of soldiers to 300. It was going to be clear who had the power.

So, it is with us today. We often think that all of our power is our own. We are sometimes very arrogant about what we have done. Meekness means to have confidence in the power we have without being arrogant. Can you take a moment today to think about where your own strength comes from?

Notes:

Matthew 5:6

Hunger and Thirst

*⁶ Blessed are those who hunger and thirst for
righteousness,
For they shall be filled.*

Sarah sits at the outer edge of the multitudes,
listening to the traveling rabbi, Jesus. Her heart is
being warmed by His message on "Blessed." While
she has been physically poor all of her life, she is
beginning to understand what it means to be poor
in spirit, to know that she needs God in her life. She
knows what it means to mourn her own sin, as she
often contemplates her spiritual condition at the end
of the day. She knows meekness, as she tries to
model her life after her namesake, Abraham's wife.
She often imagines what it was like long ago for
Sarah to quietly trust in God's power, even when
she was a very old woman. Sarah agreed to follow
Abraham even when they did not know where God
was taking them. Much later, Sarah taught her son
Isaac what it meant to hunger and thirst for
righteousness.

Now Jesus is talking about hunger and thirst. An
empty belly and a parched throat, that is something
that Sarah is very familiar with. However, this is a
different kind of hunger and thirst, this is a hunger
and thirst for righteousness, for being right with
God. Jesus says that God can fill this need.

Sarah remembers a Psalm that they often sing, "As
the deer pants for the water brooks, so pants my

203

soul for You, O God. My soul thirsts for God, for the living God" (Psalm 42:1-2a). She begins to see what Jesus is talking about, about thirsting for the living God. She begins to see how the spiritual pieces fit together. We first have to know our own spiritual poverty, then we have to mourn over our own spiritual condition. We have to really want to be right with God, like a deer pants for water at the clear running brook.

When we get to the place where we really want God, to trust Him with our whole life, then He will fill us. This rabbi gives Sarah a lot to think about.

So, it is with us. Do you need to step back and look at your spiritual condition, your personal relationship with God? Do you really trust Him with that one thing that you have been worrying about for days? Do you thirst for His righteousness like you thirst for your favorite beverage? Is it time for you to reassess your hunger and thirst?

Notes:

Matthew 5:7

Mercy

⁷ Blessed are the merciful,
For they shall obtain mercy.

When Jesus says, "Blessed are the merciful, for they shall obtain mercy" like almost everyone else in the crowd, Sarah hears it backwards. She hears the part about obtaining mercy. She desperately wants to obtain mercy: mercy from the Roman oppressors, mercy from her creditors, and mercy from her complaining neighbors.

However, Jesus is calling his listeners to be merciful. They are the ones who need to show mercy to their neighbors. They are the ones who need to show compassion to the Roman soldiers. Jesus is really turning things upside down. But how can they be merciful when times are so tough?

Then, Sarah remembers other difficult times in the life of the nation of Israel, particularly these verses from Lamentations:

This I recall to my mind,
Therefore I have hope.
Through the LORD's mercies we are not
*   consumed,*
Because His compassions fail not.
They are new every morning;
Great is Your faithfulness.
"The LORD is my portion," says my soul,
"Therefore I hope in Him!"

The LORD is good to those who wait for Him,
To the soul who seeks Him.
It is good that one should hope and wait
  quietly
For the salvation of the LORD.
(Lamentations 3:21-26)

When the Israelites recall the LORD'S mercies, then they have hope. His compassion does not fail; in fact it is renewed each day. His faithfulness is great. Because of His faithfulness they can have hope. With this hope comes the salvation of the LORD. From this hope and salvation, mercy can grow in their hearts.

Sarah suddenly understands what Jesus is talking about. Everything starts with her heart, her relationship with God. She needs to see her need for God, her spiritual poverty. She needs to hunger and thirst for righteousness. She needs to have mercy in her heart that is new each morning. Only then will she see the salvation of the LORD and His mercy.

Can you find hope in the LORD today? Can you grab hold of His mercies that are not consumed and are new every morning?

Notes:

Matthew 5:8

Pure in Heart

⁸ Blessed are the pure in heart,
For they shall see God.

Nicodemus is a Pharisee, like his father before him. From an early age he learned about the Law and adhering to the Law and the teachings of the Pharisees. They are a strict family and they adhere to every part of the Law. Nicodemus' favorite task as a child was to prepare the tithe on their homegrown mint, anise, and cummin. Each week before the Sabbath, he would count the new mint leaves and then cut one tenth of them for the tithe. He remembered when he was a very young boy how he would often get frustrated because he would lose count and then he would have to start over again. As he grew older, he learned better ways to count the mint to prepare the tithe. He also learned many other ways to adhere to the Law and the teachings of the Pharisees. He came to believe that this is what it meant to be faithful to God.

This new, travelling rabbi, the one called Jesus, does not speak of faithfulness the same way. He says that God is more concerned with the matters of the heart than strict obedience to the teachings of the Pharisees. He talks about knowing your spiritual poverty, about mourning over your sin, and about being merciful. He does not talk about showing others your generosity by loudly announcing your giving or showing others how you pray aloud on the way to the synagogue. He does not talk about tithing at all.

He reminds Nicodemus of the teaching of Isaiah: "Inasmuch as these people draw near with their mouths and honor Me with their lips, but have removed their hearts far from Me, and their fear toward Me is taught by the commandment of men" (Isaiah 29:13).

Jesus is focusing on the attitude of the heart. He says that the pure in heart shall see God. Could it be that one does not come to personally know and trust God by adhering to every miniscule part of the Pharisee's teaching? Nicodemus begins to think about what he treasures. He begins to think about how he prays. Perhaps he should have a late-night talk with Jesus about the things of God and what it means to have a pure heart.

Is it time for you to have a late-night talk with Jesus about your heart?

Notes:

Matthew 5:9

Peacemakers

⁹ Blessed are the peacemakers,
For they shall be called sons of God.

When Eli hears Jesus talking about peace, it really gets his attention. He does not have much peace in his life. He does not have peace with his neighbors. It all started when they built their new fence just touching his property. Eli thought they should have moved it at least six inches away, but they refused. Who would have thought that a leather business would be so noisy? But the other neighbors are always pounding on the leather day and night. He has no peace with his neighbors.

He does not have peace with himself either. He is always tormented that he did not follow the path that his father set out for him. He did not want to be a lawyer. He is happy being a carpenter. But he has to admit that money is often tight and he and his wife argue about money, a lot! He often stays up late at night wondering how he can have peace in his heart and peace in his home.

He also does not have peace with God. He knows the Law, but he just cannot fully keep it. He often skimps on the tithe because money is so tight. Talk about coveting. He often dreams about having many of the nice things that almost all of his neighbors have. He can go on and on, and he often does late at night. He feels like he is in the time of Jeremiah when Jeremiah talked about the false prophets who declared "'Peace, peace!' When there was no peace" (Jeremiah 8:11).

Eli is beginning to see what this rabbi, Jesus, is talking about. Peace does not start outside of us, but inside our hearts. We must first get peace with God by confessing our sins to Him and then asking Him to take over our hearts and lives. Then, we can finally have peace with ourselves because we are doing what God wants us to do. After this, we can begin the hard work of bringing peace to those around us. When we do this, we will be adopted into God's family as His children.

Do you need peace in your heart? Can you start by confessing your sin to God and asking Him for His forgiveness and His peace? Perhaps from there you will be able to become a peacemaker. Do you want to try?

Notes:

Matthew 5:10-12

Persecution!

10 Blessed are those who are persecuted for righteousness' sake,
For theirs is the kingdom of heaven.

11 Blessed are you when they revile and persecute you, and say all kinds of evil against you falsely for My sake. 12 Rejoice and be exceedingly glad, for great is your reward in heaven, for so they persecuted the prophets who were before you.

Everyone is having an interesting time listening to this new rabbi, Jesus. He is driving home issues of the heart, knowing that we need God. He says we need to really hunger for His righteousness, we need to have merciful and pure hearts. Things are sounding pretty good until He talks about persecution.

First Jesus finishes the Beatitudes with "Blessed are those who are persecuted for righteousness' sake." Okay, maybe it is not too bad to be persecuted for being right. Perhaps this means being persecuted because you are doing the right thing that God told you to do. That sounds reasonable, but pretty harsh.

Jesus then continues with blessings for you when you are persecuted for His sake. Who does He think He is? He compares Himself with the prophets of old. Does this rabbi think that He is on the same plane as Isaiah, Jeremiah, and Ezekiel? No, He seems to be saying that He is on a higher plane. Those prophets were the ones persecuted. They were persecuted because they were doing what God told them to do. Is this Jesus putting Himself on the same plane as God Himself?

Many of the multitudes begin to store this message in their hearts. This One, Jesus, is claiming to be someone special, really special. They begin to see that you cannot describe Jesus as just a good teacher. He describes Himself in much higher terms than a good teacher. Here He is hinting at the fact that He is on the same plane as God. Later, He will claim that He is One with the Father. If this is true, He claims absolute and total obedience. On the flip side, He offers a great reward in heaven.

Who do you say that Jesus is? Just a good teacher or Lord of the universe? What do you think about being persecuted for Jesus' sake?

Notes:

Concluding Thoughts

It would have been great to walk with Jesus during His time here on the Earth. But we have something just as good: the written word of His life here in Galilee. We also have something even better: the Holy Spirit indwelling our hearts.

Can you go tell someone of the joy in your heart today?